D0398520

sentially
doing
forget-
rself ;
self it is
be firmly
ow and
one has
Second Sex

What Woman es
lacks today for
great things is
fulness of he
but to forget ones
First necessary to
assured that n
for the future
found oneself The

MOTHER
was not a
person

compiled by
Margret Andersen

HQ
1457
.A62

Copyright Canada 1972 by Margret Andersen. All rights reserved. No part of this book may be reproduced or transmitted in any form, by any means, electronical or mechanical, including photocopying, without written permission from the publisher or editor (in concert with the appropriate contributors), except for use by a reviewer or a commentator in a newspaper, magazine, television or radio. Reprint fees negotiable. When reprints applicable, adequate identification of source mandatory. Published jointly by Content Publishing Limited and Black Rose Books of Montreal.
Orders:
  Mother Was Not a Person
  Suite 404
  1411 Crescent Street
  Montreal 107, Que.

  272 pages, $3.95

I-2/
b-2/

CONTENTS

59583

III. WOMEN AND THE ARTS: CRITICISM AND POETRY

IV. WOMEN AND THEIR BODIES

Acknowledgements

Grateful acknowledgement is made to the following:

H. E. MacDermot, for permission to quote from *Maude Abbott*; Byrne Hope Sanders for permission to quote from *Emily Murphy, Crusader*;

The University of Toronto Press for permission to quote from Nellie McClung, *In Times Like These;*

Editions du Jour for permission to quote from Thérèse Casgrain, *Une Femme chez les Hommes;*

The *McGill Journal of Education,* for permission to reprint the article by Margaret Gillett, *The Becoming of Caroline;*

The *Montreal Star* for permission to reprint an article by Janet Kask, "Women and the Law",

Anansi, for permission to quote from Margaret Atwood, *Power Politics* as well as from *The Circle Game* by Margaret Atwood;

Oxford University Press for permission to quote from Margaret Atwood's books, *The Animals in That Country, Procedures for Under Ground, The Journals of Susanna Moodie;*

Harper & Row for permission to quote from Nancy Milford, *Zelda;*

Viewpoints for permission to reprint a poem by Inge Packer;

Our Generation for permission to reprint an article by Lucia Kowaluk, *"Commentary* on the Status of Women Report",

Little, Brown (Boston) for permission to quote from Norman Mailer, *Of a Fire on The Moon;*

The Philosophy Department of the State University College, Fredonia, N.Y., for permission to print the article by Christine Garside, "Women and Persons".

DEDICATION

— Nellie McClung (1873-1951), the most aggressive and most witty of the Canadian suffragettes, published in 1916 a book called *In Times Like These*. At the beginning of her book, we find two dedications which seem at their place also at the beginning of this present book:

DEDICATION
I

To the Superior Person

Who would not come to hear a woman speak, being firmly convinced that it is not "natural;"

Who take the rather unassailable ground that "men are men and women are women;"

Who answer all arguments by saying, "Woman's place is the home," and "The hand that rocks the cradle rules the world," and even sometimes flash out with the brilliant retort, "It would suit those women better to stay at home and darn their children's stockings" —

To all these Superior Persons, men and women, who are inhospitable to new ideas, and even suspicious of them, this book is respectfully dedicated by

The Author.

Upon further deliberation I am beset with the fear that the above dedication may not "take." The Superior Person may not appreciate the kind and neighborly spirit I have tried to show. So I will dedicate this book again.

DEDICATION
II

Believing that the woman's claim to a common humanity is not an unreasonable one, and that the successful issue of such claim rests primarily upon the sense of fair play which people have or have not according to how they were born; and

Believing that the man or woman born with a sense of fair play, no matter how obscured it has become by training, prejudice or unhappy experience, will ultimately see the light and do the square thing; and

Believing that the man or woman who has not been so endowed by nature, no matter what their advantages of education or association have been, will always suffer from the affliction known as mental strabismus, over which no feeble human word has any power, and which can only be cast out by the transforming power of God's grace.

Therefore to men and women everywhere who love a fair deal, and are willing to give it to everyone, even women, this book is respectfully dedicated by the author.

Nellie L. McClung.

PREFACE

This anthology of writings by Montreal women comes as the result of a course on Women in Modern Society which I coordinated, in 1971/72, at Loyola of Montreal.

Fifty students (45 women, 5 men) had registered in the course. The men lived through it, handed in good work, but remained passive members of a rather active group, finding themselves in a position which is usually held by women. Three of the women dropped the course after a few sessions; one woman hated every moment and every aspect of it, making it quite clear to all of us but herself that she was afraid to become conscious of a need for liberation. But she stayed, always defending femininity with ardour. I give her credit for her stamina and hope she looks at this book.

To see the interesting work that some of the students were producing confirmed me in my belief that term papers or essays ought not to be a private matter between student and teacher only, but ought to be available to other interested people. I decided to start collecting material for an anthology.

It had also become evident to us that there are only very few Canadian publications on women. Of course, Canadian women became persons in 1929 only, when His Majesty's Privy Council in London, having received a petition from five energetic Canadian women, overruled, after four days of debate, the Supreme Court of Canada which had decided in 1928 that, under the British North America Act of 1867, women were not persons.

An anthology, as I had planned it, would first of all allow some Canadian women to say their particular say about themselves and would also find its place among Canadian feminist writings

1

which will, I have no doubt, become more and more numerous and significant.

The women in the course varied greatly as to age, background, and social position. Some were not even twenty, others were over fifty. Some were students, both graduate and undergraduate, some were professional or business women. Some were homemakers. All the variations of marital status were represented.

The interdisciplinary approach that I had chosen for the course brought us into contact with well-known American and Canadian feminists, as well as with not so widely known feminists of the Montreal area. Consequently, the idea of an anthology of students' writings progressed to that of an anthology of writings by Montreal women.

Because of the diversity of its contributors, the contents of the book vary as to quality and style. I would ask the reader to accept the fact that a number of contributors are neither professional writers nor professional women, but are women, young or old, who are slowly, but with enthusiasm, learning to understand and to express themselves. The testimony of such emergence seemed to me worthwhile recording. The book also lacks completeness. I do in no way wish to imply that it contains all that Montreal women have to say. Many women in our city will find that they could have added to what we thought pertinent, others will regret that the book is published in English and contains very few articles by Québécois women.

The book risks being called reactionary and rightly so. It is a middle-class publication which will be read by middle-class women; it will serve middle-class purposes. The myth of sisterhood, of a sisterhood of all women, will, as Marlene Dixon explains in her analysis of the feminist movement, remain a myth and a myth which is doomed to collapse. I wish for better, but am forced to accept my own limitations: I am a middle-class woman living in a middle-class environment; I will not bring about *The Revolution*. But I can, in my own middle-class way, further social change, further the acceptance of it. And certainly, I can learn. My involvement in women's studies has shown me how much there is for me to learn, about myself and about the unknown 51% of the human race. This is why my liberal or reactionary feminism is better than no feminism, why, indeed, such feminism is necessary. The Royal Commission Report states that "no prejudice in human society is so deeply embedded or so little understood" as the prejudice against women. A transformation of society's attitude "will be achieved only as a conse-

2

quence of a continuing study of the position of women in society and continuous efforts to secure justice and equal opportunity.''

What did our small group of fifty people learn in 1971/72? We have learned to appreciate other women and ourselves, we have acquired knowledge of the past and present history of women, of their role in society, of ourselves. This knowledge may in due course help us to attain what Simone de Beauvoir defines as the basic condition of true creativity: forgetfulness of one's self, possible only after one has found oneself.

We have, I believe, acquired the 'courage to see' as Mary Daly puts it, and are now in a position to claim the freedom to be, to be ourselves. May this book, which I present with pride and with fear (the feminine inferiority complex dies hard), assist just a few women in their search for themselves and may they — hopefully Marlene Dixon will forgive us — spread the word: SISTERHOOD IS BEAUTIFUL.

Margret Andersen

WOMEN'S PLACE:
how it was

Examples of Early Canadian Feminism

> Without aggression, without any noisy obtrusiveness,
> a few Canadian women by deep thought, by clear
> vision, or by honest service have prepared the way
> for those who will follow, and have proved the right
> of all to work as they are able.
>
> *Carrie M. Derrick, 1900*

Henrietta Muir Edwards (1849-1933), organizer of the Montreal Working Girls Association (1875), editor of the paper *The Working Woman of Canada*, member of the National Council of Women, author of two books on the legal status of women, suffragette, contributed in 1900 an essay on "The Political Position of Canadian Women" to the report on *Women in Canada*, compiled by the National Council of Women of Canada, which the Canadian government was to distribute at the Exposition Mondiale, in Paris. Following is one excerpt; it sounds modest but firm, a characteristic of Henrietta Muir Edwards:

Many of the statesmen of the Anglo-Saxon race, who stand higher than their fellows, and scan the political horizon, see in the distance the sure coming of the enfranchisement of women. Some of the leaders, such as Lord Salisbury, would welcome the woman's vote as a factor for good in the politics of England. In Canada, Sir John A. Macdonald went so far as to insert a clause conferring the franchise on widows and spinsters in his Franchise Bill of 1883, but public opinion was so strongly against it at that time that he withdrew it.

Canadian women themselves, until lately, have taken very little interest in this movement, and a few years ago, were, as a whole, antagonistic to it. However, at the present time almost every Canadian woman, who is at all interested in questions of the day dealing with education, philanthropy, or social life, is in favor of some form of woman franchise, either school, municipal, or parliamentary. This rapid change of opinion and its causes make an interesting study. The higher education of women, their organized efforts to ameliorate the condition of the poor, or benefit the community, their position in the labour market necessitating laws to protect their interests and welfare, have taught our women that on this account it would be well to have a direct influence upon those who govern. Personal

7

influence, of which we hear so much and which, in its place, is powerful, is very slow in action. The woman is queen in her home and reigns there, but unfortunately the laws she makes reach no further than her domain. If her laws, written or unwritten, are to be enforced outside, she must come into the political world as well ...

In the same volume, Marie Gérin-Lajoie (1867-1945), Montreal author, one of the founders of the Fédération Nationale Saint Jean Baptiste, and also a suffragette, concludes her essay on "The Legal Status of Women in the Province of Quebec" with a quiet appeal to the Quebec people and a politely worded threat against the legal system:

> ... it may be concluded from this article on the legal status of woman, that, as far as she is concerned, in all cases, except in simple administrative acts that are permitted her when she is separate as to property, the wife, without her husband's authorization is incapable of performing any acts whatsoever of importance, that might tend to the acquiring of new property, or the alienation of her capital. She cannot increase her responsibilities without the concurrence and agreement of the one to whom she has devoted her life.
>
> In general the woman exercises her activity in a sphere of action more restricted than the limits traced by the hand of the law. In truth it is only, as it were, by exception and on isolated occasions in her existence that she touches the confines of an ever-increasing domain. But the law is unbending, and only becomes more generous after reiterated assaults, and when the impression of customs make it clear that it must expand and progress.

Again in the same volume, the first president (1893-1899) of the National Council of Women of Canada, Ishbel Countess of Aberdeen, defines the aims and achievements of the Council as follows:

> 1. It obtained the introduction of manual training and the instruction in domestic science in the public schools of Ontario, and the training of teachers, so that they may be able to give instruction in these arts. It has also given an emphasis to the same movement in other provinces.
>
> 2. It has obtained the appointment of Women Factory Inspectors for factories and workshops where women are employed, in the Provinces of Quebec and Ontario.
>
> 3. It has obtained the extension of the provisions of the Factory Act to the Shops Act in Ontario as regards the supervision of women workers, and is taking steps to promote the same extension in the Province of Quebec.
>
> 4. It has obtained the appointment of women on the Boards of

School Trustees in New Brunswick, and the amendment of the School Act so that they may be elected in British Columbia. It has also compiled a report on the regulations and methods of electing members of School Boards in all the seven Provinces in which much variety exists.

5. It has brought about very desirable changes in the arrangements for women prisoners in various places, notably in the City of Quebec, where matrons are now in charge of the women, and young girls are now sent to a separate institution.

6. It has organized in various centres Boards of Associated Charities, or other systems of co-operation in the relief of distress, and is still working in this direction wherever it has opportunity so to do, and has circulated a valuable paper on the problem of the unemployed.

7. It has established Hospitals in some of its smaller centres.

8. It originated the idea of the Victorian Order of Nurses, and has taken a leading part in its establishment in different centres.

9. It has organized Cooking Schools, Cooking Classes, and at Quebec is helping in the formation of a Training School for Domestic Servants.

10. It has spread sanitary knowledge, especially by means of Health Talks for Mothers, given by physicians in Montreal. This has been specially successful both amongst the French and English mothers.

11. It has held an enquiry all over the country into the circulation of impure literature, and has been able to do something to lessen it already, as well as to warn parents and teachers as to the very great danger that exists in this direction. It hopes to be able to do more by legislation and by the circulation of healthy and interesting literature.

12. It inaugurated the National Home Reading Union to promote habits of good and systematic reading, and this Union is making most satisfactory progress.

13. It instituted enquiries into the conditions surrounding working women in several centres, and urges on its members various methods whereby they may work for their amelioration.

14. It conducted an enquiry in all the Provinces into the Laws for the Protection of Women and Children, and laid certain recommendations before the Minister of Justice, which he adopted when bringing in amendments to the Criminal Law in 1899. These amendments did not become law because of lack of time for their final consideration, but the Council has again pledged itself earnestly to support their adoption.

15. It is earnestly concerning itself in the care and treatment of the aged poor, and also of the feeble-minded.

16. It calls on all its members to unite in efforts for the protection of animal and bird life from useless destruction in the interests of fashion.

17. Through one of its affiliated societies it is endeavoring to plan for the better care and wiser distribution of women immigrants than has hitherto been possible, and in the case of the Doukhoborts it has provided the women with materials for carrying on home industries and other much-needed assistance for their first winter in Canada.

18. It is pledged to co-operate with medical authorities in urging immediate measures to be taken to check the ever increasing ravages of consumptive diseases in this country; to spread knowledge on the subject, and bring responsibility home to individuals.

19. It desires to promote the systematic instruction in Art Design adaptable to Industries and Manufactures, as opening up a field full of opportunities for women.

20. On several occasions the pressing needs of the women and children of a city partially destroyed by sudden fire, have been relieved at a few hours' notice, by the combined action of a Council of women in a neighbouring city, whose organization gave it the opportunity to render prompt and efficient help.

21. At the desire of the Red Cross Society, it is now organizing Branches of this Society all over Canada, for the relief of sufferers in the War.

22. At the request of the Dominion Government it has compiled this Hand-book of information on matters relating to Canadian women and their work, for publication and distribution at the Paris Exhibition, at the expense of the Government.

It is interesting to see how Maude Abbott (1869-1940), one of the first women M.D.'s in Quebec, longed to be educated in the company of other women and how she questioned her own abilities. The following excerpts from her diary are quoted from her biography written by H. E. MacDermot[1]:

March, 1884. One of my day-dreams, which I feel to be selfish, is that of going to school. I know Alice would like it herself ever so much, but I do so *long* to go. And here I go again; once begin dreaming of the possibilities and I become half daft over what I know will never come to pass. Oh, to *think* of studying with other girls! Think of learning German, Latin, and other languages in general. Think of the loveliness of thinking that it entirely depended on myself whether I got on ...

March 29, 1884. Lillie told me my fortune last night, and said I was to get my wish. My wish! Oh, if I were to get it: if that *were* to come true (though of course I don't believe in fortune-telling by cards) — but if I *were* to go to school, if it were only for one term, how happy I would be. I don't think it is the other girls' society I want, or anything of that sort, but the good education I would love — how I long for one.

April 1, 1884. I wonder what my life will be like, and if I will have any opportunity to do something good or great with it ... How can anyone think anything nice about me? It must be that they don't know me well enough ...

I feel taken down again in my estimate of myself, perhaps too much so, as everyone should respect themselves to a certain point, to which I do not reach. I wonder whether I feel like this simply because I have a toothache and am feeling generally out of sorts. Dr. Holland says the need of a 'blue pill' often brings on these morbid feelings. I certainly have a fit of the 'blues' today ...

April 9. I have been thinking so much about going to school next winter. I can't help building these castles in the air, selfish as I know them to be. I wonder if there is the faintest chance of my doing so? I have wondered and wondered until I am perfectly sick of it, yet can't stop. I am sure I wouldn't waste my time, at least I would study hard and not throw time away. I could scarcely help improving the shining hour while it lasted — if it ever does come to pass and I get my wish I will try to keep my resolutions (1) to study hard and conscientiously; (2) not to get wild, etc., as many girls do; (3) not to care for the competition, but for the real study and the benefit I will derive from it; (4) to remember that I go to school for education, not for fun.

June 25. When I come to turn myself over and pick myself to pieces, it is really awful how few lovable points I have in my character. I am half convinced I am clever since Nellie argued the point with me, but my idea of cleverness is entirely different from what I am. I have a good memory, but because I have that I cannot see why I should be clever ... I always know my lessons — put that down to a good memory and a desire to get on. Now, what else is clever in me? I am no hand at all at conversation and invariably spoil a good story in the telling. I certainly never come out with dry clever things, in fact I never make any bright remarks. I have not read much at all, or that might give a clever tinge to me.

Dec. 28, 1884. It is over a month since I last wrote here, and I am just jotting down a few lines to tell how my wish has come true, and I have gone to school, so now I have a chance to keep those resolutions I made a few pages back, and better still am in a fair way to do so.

We are never satisfied. My next wish is to go to college, and now I am wishing for that almost as ardently as I did last winter for my present good fortune. I wonder what I shall do if I am plucked in June?

On May 15, 1909, a newspaper, *The Montreal Witness,* published a Women's Edition, edited by women only. It is a rather tame edition which does not really touch upon the question of women's rights. However, it does contain one letter to the editor which shows that this question was indeed a burning one.

11

THE BURNING QUESTION
(To the Editor of the 'Daily Witness')

Madam, — (In the exuberance of my spirits I had almost called you 'dear friend.')

This is the time of our life, and my only regret is that the knowledge of this privilege did not come to us earlier: otherwise we might have arranged for a 'coup d-état'!

If we would succeed against the treachery of man, we must fight him with his own weapon; we must overthrow his rule over night; the castle must be stormed whilst the guard sleeps!

You see, dear friend and editor, I speak my mind freely. I could not have done so to an egotistical male editor. Why not, it strikes me, why not establish our own Press everywhere, and henceforth speak our minds unrestrainedly on the subject of Women's Rights. I see no obstacles — whatever other, narrow-minded woman may do. I am referring to Clarissa, who asked me yesterday on whose money we were to run our Press. She wanted to know whether we would deign to do so on the money allotted to our housekeeping, or on the pin-money allowed us by our husbands or fathers, or on what had been bequeathed us by our fathers, uncles, or brothers — or for the matter of that, on any men's money.

I feel no such petty scruples. Who is it, I ask, who seeks to kill every business instinct in us? Who ridicules our efforts when we try early and late to buy cheaply at the annual bargain counters? — and who, but man? I have always nourished my business instincts. When John puts a quarter behind his plate as a tip to the waiter — when we are dining alone — it is I who replace it with a ten-cent piece and so demonstrate my better commercial talents.

'How, if not on man's money, are we to begin to work out our redemption,' I asked Clarissa. And what do you suppose she answered? She said we were to earn the capital. 'Earn it,' she said, 'but not in the capacities in which we were generally and preferentially employed by men: as canvassers for subscriptions for educational works — among men; as bill-collectors, as collectors for charities — among men; as mistresses of ceremony in photographers' studios, as programme sellers and theatre attendants, as stenographers in offices, and, in short, in the dozen and one capacities where pleasing exteriors and no brains were demanded. 'Instead,' Clarissa continued, 'if we thought ourselves wise enough to relieve man in part of his onerous duties in business and state, we should demonstrate our maturity by crediting some of our own number with more profundity, more genius, more justice and more disinterestedness of spirit than we do or have done hitherto; we should with broader minds, more charity and more loyalty give our aid and countenance wholeheartedly to those who, prepared and full of conviction of the necessity, desire and attempt to open honourable and earnest walks of life (in no measure and no wise inferior to those followed by man) to those of their sisters who from one or other of the many causes growing out of the evils of the day find that they must abandon the prime destiny of their sex and battle for their existence.'

I agreed that we might be wise enough to help govern, but that we were scarcely strong enough to forge huge beams and shafts after the manner of men. But Clarissa would allow none of my objections. She maintained that, already and daily, more large electric furnaces and machinery, instinct with all but intelligence, and demanding no more attention than women could bestow, performed these tasks for man. 'And were not women engaged in occupations that robbed them of health and life and claimed their thousands in death yearly?' she argued.

In conclusion ... but dear editor, I find that the gladsome note I struck at the beginning of this letter has given place to one of earnestness and dejection. Am I then wrong? Would a coup d'état have been out of place? Must we then build up a world of our own in the midst of the existing one? Or shall we retain the role of make-believe-importance we have played from time immemorial for the benefit of man? Shall we henceforth be grave or gay?

ARABELLA RICHARDS.

We must be grateful to Veronica Strong-Boag for having presented us with a new edition of Nellie McClung's *In Times Like These*,[2] for Nellie McClung, (1874-1951), writer and activist, deserves to be more widely known. Her book is a feminist manifesto of great wit, as the following excerpts show:

Prejudices:

If prejudices belonged to the vegetable world they would be described under the general heading of: "Hardy Perennials; will grow in any soil and bloom without ceasing; require no cultivation; will do better when left alone."

... Take some of the prejudices regarding women that have been exploded and blown to pieces many, many times and yet walk among us today in the fulness of life and vigor. There is a belief that housekeeping is the only occupation for women; that all women must be housekeepers, whether they like it or not. Men do as they like ... but every true and womanly woman must take to the nutmeg grater and the O-Cedar mop ....

Feminism:

We may as well admit that there is discontent among women ... But there is really no cause for alarm, for discontent is not necessarily wicked. There is such a thing as divine discontent ... In the old days, when a woman's hours were from 5 A.M. to 5 A.M., we did not hear much of discontent among women, because they had no time to even talk and certainly could not get together. The horse

13

on the treadmill may be very discontented, but he is not disposed to tell, for he cannot stop to talk.

It is the women, who now have leisure, who are doing the talking. For generations, women have been thinking, and thought without expression is dynamic and gathers volume by repression. Evolution when blocked and suppressed becomes revolution.

The Vote:

Women have dispensed charity for many, many years, but gradually it has dawned upon them that the most of our charity is very ineffectual and merely smoothes things over, without ever reaching the root ... If women would only be content to snip away at the symptoms of poverty and distress, feeding the hungry and clothing the naked, all would be well and they would be much commended for their kindness of heart; but when they begin to inquire into causes, they find themselves in the sacred realm of politics where prejudice says no woman must enter ...

Now politics simply mean public affairs — yours and mine, everybody's — and to say that politics are too corrupt for women is a weak and foolish statement for any man to make. Any man who is actively engaged in politics, and declares that politics are too corrupt for women, admits one of two things, either that he is a party to this corruption or that he is unable to prevent it — and in either case something should be done ... Women have cleaned up things since time began; and if women ever get into politics there will be a cleaning-out of pigeon-holes and forgotten corners, on which the dust of years has fallen, and the sound of the political carpet-beater will be heard in the land.

There is another hardy perennial that constantly lifts its head above the earth ... and that is that if women were ever given a chance to participate in outside affairs, family quarrels would result ... If a husband and wife are going to quarrel they will find a cause for dispute easily enough, and will not be compelled to wait for election day ...

In spite of the testimony of many reputable women that they have been able to vote and get the dinner on one and the same day, there still exists a strong belief that the whole household machinery gets out of order when a women goes to vote. No person denies a woman the right to go to church, and yet the church service takes a great deal more time than voting ...

People are indifferent about many things that they should be interested in. The indifference of people on the subject of ventilation and hygiene does not change the laws of health. The indifference of many parents on the subject of an education for their children does not alter the value of education. If one woman wants to vote, she should have that opportunity just as if one woman desires a college education, she should not be held back because of the indifferent careless ones who do not desire it. Why should the mentally inert, careless, uninterested woman, who cares nothing for humanity but is contented to patter along her own little narrow way, set the pace for the others of us? Voting will not be compulsory; the shrinking violets will not be torn from their shady fence-corner; the "home bodies" will be able to still sit in rapt contemplation of their own fireside. We will not force the vote upon them, but why should they force their votelessness upon us?

The Law:

It is a hard matter, I know, to protect people from themselves; and there can be no law made to prevent women from making slaves of themselves to their husbands and families. That would be interfering with the sanctity of the home! But the law can step in, as it has in some provinces, and prevent a man from leaving his wife with only "her keep." The law is a reflection of public sentiment, and when people begin to realize that women are human and have human needs and ambitions and desires, the law will protect a woman's interest. Too long we have had this condition of affairs: "Ma" has been willing to work without any recompense, and "Pa and the boys" have been willing to let her.

Of course, I know, sentimental people will cry out, that very few men would leave their wives in poverty — I know that; men are infinitely better than the law, but we must remember that laws are not made to govern the conduct of good men. Good men will do what is right, if there were never a law; but, unfortunately, there are some men who are not good, and many more who are thoughtless and unintentionally cruel. The law is a schoolmaster to such.

Economics:

There was a rich farmer once, who died possessed of three very fine farms of three hundred and twenty acres each. He left a farm to each of his three sons. To his daughter Martha, a woman of forty years of age, the eldest of the family, who had always stayed at home, and worked for the whole family — he left a cow and one hundred dollars. The wording of the will ran: "To my dear daughter, Martha, I leave the sum of one hundred dollars, and one cow named 'Bella.' "

How would you like to be left at forty years of age, with no training and very little education, facing the world with one hundred dollars and one cow, even if she were named "Bella?"

The Church:

Woman has long been regarded by the churches as helpmate for man, with no life of her own, but a very valuable assistant nevertheless to some male relative. Woman's place they have long been told is to help some man to achieve success and great reward may be hers. Some day when she is faded and old and battered and bent, her son may be pleased to recall her many sacrifices and declare when making his inaugural address: "All that I am my mother made me!" There are one or two things to be considered in this charming scene. Her

15

son may never arrive at this proud achievement, or even if he does, he may forget his mother and her sacrifices, and again she may not have a son. But these are minor matters.

Children do not need their mother's care always, and the mother who has given up every hope and ambition in the care of her children will find herself left all alone when her children no longer need her — a woman without a job. But, dear me, how the church has exalted the self-sacrificing mother, who never had a thought apart from her children, and who became a willing slave to her family. Never a word about the injury she is doing to her family in letting them be a slave-owner, never a word of the injury she is doing to herself, never a whisper of the time when the children may be ashamed of their worked-out mother who did not keep up with the times.

The preaching of the church, having been done by men, has given us the strictly masculine viewpoint. The tragedy of the "willing slave, the living sacrifice," naturally does not strike a man as it does a woman. A man loves to come home and find his wife or his mother darning his socks. He likes to believe that she does it joyously. It is traditionally correct, and home would not be home without it. No man wants to stay at home too long, but he likes to find his women folks sitting around when he comes home. The stationary female and the wide-ranging male is the world's accepted arrangement, but the belief that a woman must cherish no hope or ambition of her own is both cruel and unjust.

Marriage:

The world has never been partial to the thinking woman — the wise ones have always foreseen danger. Long years ago, when women asked for an education, the world cried out that it would never do. If women learned to read it would distract them from the real business of life which was to make home happy for some good man. If women learned to read there seemed to be a possibility that some day some good man might come home and find his wife reading, and the dinner not ready — and nothing could be imagined more horrible than that! That seems to be the haunting fear of mankind — that the advancement of women will sometime, someway, someplace, interfere with some man's comfort. There are many people who believe that the physical needs of her family are a woman's only care; and that strict attention to her husband's wardrobe and meals will insure a happy marriage. Hand-embroidered slippers warmed and carefully set out have ever been highly recommended as a potent charm to hold masculine affection. They forget that men and children are not only food-eating and clothes-wearing animals — they are human beings with other and even greater needs than food and raiment.

Any person who believes that the average man marries the woman of his choice just because he wants a housekeeper and a cook, appraises mankind lower than I do. Intelligence on the wife's part does not destroy connubial bliss, neither does ignorance nor apathy ever make

16

for it. Ideas do not break up homes, but lack of ideas. The light and airy silly fairy may get along beautifully in the days of courtship, but she palls a bit in the steady wear and tear of married life.

There was a picture in one of the popular woman's papers sometime ago, which taught a significant lesson. It was a breakfast scene. The young wife, daintily frilled in pink, sat at her end of the table in very apparent ill-humor — the young husband, quite unconscious of her, read the morning paper with evident interest. Below the picture there was a sharp criticism of the young man's neglect of his pretty wife and her dainty gown. Personally I sympathize with the young man and believe it would be a happier home if she were as interested in the paper as he and were reading the other half of it instead of sitting around feeling hurt.

The time will come, we hope, when women will be economically free, and mentally and spiritually independent enough to refuse to have their food paid for by men; when women will receive equal pay for equal work, and have all avenues of activity open to them; and will be free to choose their own mates, without shame or indelicacy; when men will not be afraid of marriage because of the financial burden, but free men and free women will marry for love, and together work for the sustenance of their families. It is not too ideal a thought. It is coming, and the new movement among women who are crying out for a larger humanity is going to bring it about.

Work:

These tender-hearted and chivalrous gentlemen who tell you of their adoration for women, cannot bear to think of women occupying public positions. Their tender hearts shrink from the idea of women lawyers or women policemen, or even women preachers; these positions would "rub the bloom off the peach," to use their own eloquent words. They cannot bear, they say, to see women leaving the sacred precincts of home — and yet their offices are scrubbed by women who do their work while other people sleep — poor women who leave the sacred precincts of home to earn enough to keep the breath of life in them, who carry their scrub-pails home, through the deserted streets, long after the cars have stopped running. They are exposed to cold, to hunger, to insult — poor souls — is there any pity felt for them? Not that we have heard of. The tender-hearted ones can bear this with equanimity. It is the thought of women getting into comfortable and well-paid positions which wrings their manly hearts.

Emily Murphy (1868-1933), known also as the writer Janey Canuck, became in 1916 the first magistrate of the newly created women's court in Edmonton where, during the first months in office, she was regularly harassed by one particular lawyer who objected to her jurisdiction on the grounds that a woman is not a "person" under the British North America Act of 1867. Emily Murphy nevertheless proceeded with her work. The same argument was used to prevent women from being appointed to the Senate, but Emily Murphy, with Nellie McClung, Louise McKinney, Irene Parlby, and Henrietta Muir Edwards, petitioned "for an order in council directing the Supreme Court of Canada to rule on a constitutional point in the B.N.A. Act."[3] In 1928, the Supreme Court ruled that women were not eligible for appointment to the Senate. Disappointed, so to speak, the five women requested "an order in council giving them leave to appeal to His Majesty's Privy Council in London." The Privy Council ruled, in 1929, after four days of debate

> that the word persons includes members of the male and female sex ... and that women are eligible to be summoned and become members of the Senate of Canada.[4]

In 1931, Mackenzie King finally appointed a woman senator, Cairine Wilson.

The following statements about motherhood by Emily Murphy are taken from Byrne Hope Sanders' biography, *Emily Murphy, Crusader,*[5]:

> Although barely twenty years of age when I became a mother, I can see, in looking back across the years, that the finest joys of life came with my children: so close they are to one's heart, these younglings, and so dear.
>
> In the outside world, argue as you may concerning the proper placing of titular decorations, in the home, the habit of wearing the heart on one's sleeve is unquestionably correct as well as deeply wise.
>
> Looking back, I can see also that the so-called 'hardships' of rearing children are largely imaginative. For this reason I find it difficult to sympathize with those persons who are ever wont to dilate upon the 'tears' and 'sacrifices' of motherhood. I even find it hard to become enraptured over Mother's Day, in that the strain running through most of the editorials is one of pity and commiseration for the apparently sad and serious woman who has reared a family ... There are the florist's advertisements too. Don't forget the mode. Pink carnation if she's alive; white if she's dead.
>
> In art, the mother with a grown-up family is usually portrayed with folded hands, a resigned-to-the-inevitable air, and in a gown that is drearily suggestive of a shroud. If you wish to see this down-daunted type in its full perfection, pray study that widely known, but objectionable picture entitled "Whistler's Mother."
>
> It is my opinion and I hope that you will agree with me, that there is no reason for burning incense to a woman simply because she has fulfilled the natural functions of her sex — because she has been no skulker of her maternal responsibility.

This type of down-daunted mother is rapidly passing out, for we are coming to see that a mother who lets herself subside into a kind of burnt-sacrifice upon what is called the 'family altar' is not really a good mother, nor a good citizen.

Emily Murphy wrote on the subject of work in *The Canadian Home Journal*, in April, 1932:

The very best of business men make the family garden, tend the furnace, paint the kitchen floor, turn the washer, hang pictures, and even care for the children. Because they do both, it does not necessarily follow that either their homes or their business is neglected. And even so, marriage and motherhood need not be a hindrance but rather an inspiration to industrial or professional work — this, presuming the woman has the physical ability.

Women who learn to manage a business, observing its hours, routine, necessity for promptness, restraint, efficiency and economy, are bound to bring these qualifications to the better management of their homes. Besides the qualifications she has she inevitably improves her home by bringing to it the riches of mind which should always come from experience and a broadened outlook . . . .

The only truly contented women, are those who have both a home and a profession!

In her book on drug addiction, called *The Black Candle*,[6] we find the following phrase which seems like the leitmotif of Emily Murphy's thinking: "No woman may become or remain degraded without all women suffering . . . ."

Thérèse Casgrain is to be considered the leader of the Quebec suffrage movement. It is to a large extent due to her patient efforts that Quebec women obtained the franchise in 1940. Due to her vigilance and diplomacy, it was decided to make payment of family allowances to mothers, in Quebec, and not to fathers, as it had originally been planned. She has written her auto-biography, *Une Femme chez les Hommes*,[7] from which I quote:

A l'heure actuelle, c'est une joie de constater que partout au Canada, la relève s'organise. A tous les paliers, les autorités s'inquiètent davantage des conditions de vie des masses. L'éducation, la santé, le travail, sont devenus des sujets de préoccupation générale. Un plus grand nombre de citoyens, me semble-t-il, cherchent à participer activement à la vie politique en plus de vivement s'intéresser à ce qui se passe dans les autres pays. Mes impressions sont-elles bien fondées? J'ose répondre dans l'affirmative, du moins quant à la question du rôle des femmes dans la vie sociale. Au temps des suffragettes, ce n'était qu'une minorité de femmes qui œuvraient, la conscience ouverte non seulement à leurs propres problèmes, mais aux problèmes de la société toute entière.

Aujourd'hui, les femmes n'ont pas à envisager les mêmes difficultés qu'autrefois; elles s'affirment davantage et sont un peu mieux écoutées, mais la société d'égalité entre les hommes et les femmes est loin d'être réalisée. Tout ma vie, j'ai préconisé qu'il fallait questionner, prendre position et agir. Donc, j'approuve, en général, le courant de la libération des femmes qui s'amorce un peu partout, quoique je diffère d'opinion sur certaines modalités prises par quelques groupements de femmes pour atteindre ce but. Notre cause n'est sûrement pas renforcée parce que des milliers d'entre elles jettent non pas leur bonnet par-dessus les moulins mais leur soutien-gorge dans la rue. D'ailleurs, cet aspect peu sérieux se reflète même dans certaines des discussions de nos législateurs. Quel avantage y a-t-il à s'interroger pour savoir si, au Parlement du Canada ou dans les assemblées législatives, les jeunes filles devraient être acceptées comme pages et, dans l'affirmative, comment elles devraient être vêtues? Il est beaucoup plus important de s'attacher à des questions fondamentales, par exemple, la parité de salaire, l'égalité dans les avantages économiques et la présence des femmes dans les conseils d'administration, dans les commissions royales et dans les parlements.

Même les quelques pas en avant faits par la femme dans la voie de son émancipation ne l'empêchent pas de rester prisonnière d'une foule de préjugés. Nous sommes en face d'une société qui a besoin de se débarrasser de ses vieux concepts de racisme, de violence et de snobisme. Nous craignons trop d'abandonner les manières de voir d'autrefois quand le patriotisme signifiait l'obéissance, l'âge mûr la sagesse et la femme l'abdication. La véritable libération de la femme ne pourra pas se faire sans celle de l'homme. Au fond, le mouvement de la libération des femmes n'est pas uniquement féministe d'inspiration, il est aussi humaniste. Que les hommes et les femmes se regardent honnêtement et qu'ils essayent ensemble de revaloriser la société. Le défi auquel nous, femmes et hommes, avons à faire face, est celui de vivre pour une révolution pacifique et non pas de mourir pour une révolution cruelle et, en définitive, illusoire.

Notes

1. MacMillan, Toronto, 1941.
2. Michael Bliss, editor, University of Toronto Press, Toronto, 1972.
3. Mary Quayle Innis, *The Clear Spirit,* Canadian Federation of University Women, University of Toronto Press, Toronto, 1967, p. 165.
4. *Ibid.*, p. 175.
5. MacMillan, Toronto, 1945.
6. Thomas Allen, Toronto, 1922, p. 17.
7. Editions du Jour, Montréal, 1971.

WOMEN'S PLACE:
how it is

People still speak of womanhood as if it were a disease.

Nellie McClung, 1916

i sit in the mud
       baking
  cookies
        with my womanhood.

mary melfi, 1971

A CRITICAL LOOK AT CHILDREN'S BOOKS

When first confronted with the task of 'Researching Children's Books,' many of us were not too interested. We soon discovered, however, how absolutely wrong we were. For we found out, and quite easily too, that standardized images of men and women, in the guise of 'harmless' nursery rhymes, fairy tales and children's books are being fed into the minds of youths from the time they are toddlers. The research became an exercise in awareness.

The classic stories, at least those included in North American selections, very frequently portray a beautiful but helpless young girl in distress who is rescued from her plight by a handsome young prince (Rapunsel, Sleeping Beauty, Cinderella, etc.) *Rumpelstiltskin,* for instance, tells of the miller's daughter who is summoned before the king because her "boastful father" said she could spin straw into gold. The king says she must die if she fails and marry him if she proves successful. Her life is saved by a little man [Rumpelstiltskin] who spins the straw into gold for her. The self-centered father never once has his daughter's welfare in mind. He makes no attempt to help her out of the situation in which he has placed her. The king too thinks only of personal gain. To marry the miller's daughter appears as strictly a financial venture since there is no thought of love, happiness or companionship in the tale. Should the girl be incapable of spinning gold she would be of no use to him and must die. Even her 'Saviour' acts sheerly for his own benefit. The girl has to forfeit her first child to him in payment for his spinning the straw into gold. The truly pathetic character in this tale then is the girl. While in the hands of three merciless men, all out for personal gain, she simply vegetates, absent of thought, speech or action.

25

Although in many books small boys and girls can share adventures *(Hansel and Gretel)*, the girl must remain aware of her female role (Wendy in *Peter Pan*). By adulthood, the female has given up adventuring for the home; she encourages her men to go out to fulfill their destinies. And, because of the absoluteness of sex roles, all expression of emotion is left to females.

In children's books, particularly fairy tales, there exists both a rigidity and a belittling of the woman's role. Her place is in the home, but the home is portrayed as a place to go away from, to leave in order to experience life. Thus woman is doomed to spend her life in a self-defeating position, her duty is to care for her young; theirs is to leave as soon as they can, in order to go out and experience the *real* world.

The mother image in more recent stories is equally pitiful. An example of this is to be found in *Selected Stories For Children: Go Find Rusty,* by Edith Lowe. "Rusty lived in a little house in a little town with his mother and his father. His mother was just a mother — but his father was a painter — a house painter — and Rusty thought that was the most wonderful thing in the whole world." The little boy's hero-worship for his father is the theme, while mother appears content in preparing meals and washing, assuming the role of a shadow.

Is it possible to be different? So called 'Career books' say no. Lois Lenski, in *When I Grow Up,* introduces boys to the exciting careers of sea captain, airplane pilot, policeman or doctor. A girl may choose to become a typist, store clerk, cook, singer, nurse, (not doctor). The climax comes on the final page:

> But oh a mother is best of all,
> With lots of children big and small.

Falsely portraying this most important and rewarding career for a girl is a smiling mother with a babe-in-arms, surrounded by seven happy children, obviously produced at the rate of one per year. She appears fit enough to increase the count to an even dozen, blissfully ignoring eventual problems of mental and physical exhaustion. How many little minds have already been influenced by this book, available in a public library, and are dreaming of becoming earth mothers? Mater = mother = material.

The purpose of these 'career books' is to help young people in their choice of a career, while showing these careers to be worthwhile, exciting and interesting. Here are some titles that speak for themselves: *Brad Foster, Engineer; Barbara Nichols, Fifth Grade Teacher; Karen Simms, Private Secretary; Lee Sloan,*

26

Missionary Pilot; Sandra Emerson, R.N.

Some, but very few of the children's books have diverted from the traditional, sexist lines. An example of this is *Ann Can Fly,* by Fred Phleger. In this story, a father takes his daughter flying, and teaches her to pilot the plane. This is particularly interesting because aviation is one of the most blatantly sexist industries — one in which women are the servants (glamorized and glorified as stewardesses) and the real activity, the piloting and navigating, is performed by men only. At the end of the book Ann is in a summer camp, sitting around a campfire with other girls. Perhaps her words are prophetic, not only about the flight she is describing, but about the lives these young girls will lead. "Some day you will fly," she tells them. "You will like it. You will see!"

What kind of books are being used to teach our children the basic reading skills? Readers, of course, are not books that children have chosen for themselves, they are books that most children must read. Schoolchildren cannot avoid being subjected psychologically and sociologically to their contents.

In a primer entitled *At Home and Away,* there is one section called "At Work": Daddy is out in the fields picking strawberries which he obviously has grown; Mommy is in the kitchen cleaning and preparing Daddy's strawberries. The kitchen seems to be an extension of Mother herself; in another chapter Mommy is baking cookies in the kitchen again.

In another section, the daughter is learning how to ride a bicycle, but is shown to be a helpless, bumbling idiot. She needs her brother to help her. At one moment, Daddy is shown taking both children to look at boats. Mother seems to be non-existent outside of the home. When Mother is shown again, it is only to serve ice-cream to the children. In one chapter, the girl is trying to grow flowers by the window-sill. Of course, she is helpless again, so the boys go out to buy a flower for her to put into the flower-box. There is one scene in the entire book when mother is outside of the home — a picnic. Although she is existent this time, it is still her job to prepare the lunch, while Father goes fishing with the children.

We noticed some elements or themes common to all primary readers. In most of the books, including such books as *Dick and Jane; Janet and John,* the boy is always older and bigger than the girl, and therefore gives the impression of having more experience, knowledge and authority. There are usually two or more animals present — and even the animals are sexually stereotyped. The dog is identified with the boy, the cat is identified with the girl. The dog is more intelligent and aggressive than the cat, which is more passive and much more domesticated. In the five basal reading series that we have reviewed, the females are passive, maternal, stupid, servile, domestic, unathletic, dependent, inept, bungling, out-of-control, and unimaginative; while males are industrious, inventive, aggressive, clever, authoritative, athletic, imaginative, rugged, and capable.

In a series called *The New Basic Readers,* W. J. Gage and Co. Ltd., (No date of printing. Does this mean that they are eternal?), the central characters are Dick and Jane, 6-7 years of age, and Sally who is 3-4 years of age. The first pre-primer, *We Look and See,* shows Dick in a T-shirt and jeans watering the lawn. Baby Sally comes out wearing her father's boots and, clutching her teddy bear, loses a boot in the middle of a puddle. She is rescued by clever Dick and his red wagon. Meanwhile, Jane hugs her raggedy-Ann doll and passively observes the incident.

Next, we see Dick donning roller skates and rather cleverly harnessing Spot, the dog, and his energies. Sally says, "Look, Jane. Look, look. See Dick." Jane looks.

There's more. Poor dumb Sally drops her balloon and has it busted by Puff, the cat, whereas Dick has control over the animal world: he teaches Spot to jump over a stick.

In *We Work and Play,* also a pre-primer, we see Dick industriously painting a chair. Enter Jane with a small doll's chair in one hand and Raggedy-Ann in the other. Dick proceeds to paint the chair while Jane hugs Raggedy-Ann.

One incident in the third of the pre-primers, *We Come and Go,* shows poor Jane hopelessly trying to balance herself on a pair of roller skates. Dick is in hysterics. Sally, clutching her teddy bear, looks worried, Jane is in a panic. Good ol' Dick manages to stop laughing long enough to solve the problem by providing two broomsticks which compensate for Jane's inability to achieve balance on her own. Compare this with the roller skating episode in the first pre-primer, where Dick is not only an expert skater, but imaginative in that he uses Spot to pull him. The three primers are equally revolting. On one occasion, Dick becomes the observer while Jane shows him how she helps mother by setting the table. "Look Dick. This is for Father." (*The New Fun With Dick and Jane*). The relationship between the sexes seems summed up in the story where Dick, through imagination and invention, creates a 'car' out of a chair and a pot. "Make one for me." says Sally. Instead, Dick makes his own 'car' larger, and when Sally hesitates, he bribes her with a parasol. Whereupon she smiles, accepts the parasol and assumes the passenger seat. *(Guess Who)*.

The *Open Highways* Readers, by Scott-Foresman, 1968, have the same sexist theme running throughout the readers. Men are portrayed as steel workers, coal miners, firemen, policemen, businessmen, etc., while women are housewives, teachers and librarians. An interesting aspect of these American-published readers is that, occasionally, black people are the key characters. Needless to say, black women are portrayed to be as passive and uninteresting as the white women.

The *Canadian Reading Development* Series, Copp Clark Publishing Co. (1960, 1962), resembles the 'Dick and Jane' readers. There are three key characters, John, Janet and Anne. Anne washes her doll. Janet helps Mother bake goodies for the family, while John and Father go off on a fishing trip. *(Off to School)*. Father and John, rugged, athletic types, ski daringly down the hill while Janet and Anne take the conservative way down on sleighs. Mother isn't in on this one, but we all know where she is!

In one reader of the usual length, Mother bakes one ham, one angel cake, one custard and four pumpkin pies! Only twice is she allowed to remove her apron and step outside the home. Grandmother, also, is firmly attached to the soup kettle and the kitchen stove, while the stepmother meets a worse fate: she is being roasted in her own oven. Women's role is synonomous with kitchen activity.

But a boy has free will. It is he who is late for school or dares to arrive with his homework undone; it is only a boy who can force mother into submission. A man is able to fill two roles, his chosen career and that of a father, while a woman must remain all mother. Father reads a book or newspaper while mother, in our patriarchal society, seemingly lacks the intelligence for such activity. She sews or knits. Woman is ever submissive, ever subordinate. Miss (never Mrs.!) Miller, a secretary, trembles before an overpowering boss.

In *These Are Our Friends* (Faith and Freedom Basic Readers) father, mother, daughter and son are in character from page one to page one hundred and ninety. The children reading these stories see the father as the ruling boss figure — the decision maker, the admonisher, the breadwinner, the master over all; the mother, as portrayed even in the pictures, is the ironer, knitter, bed-maker, cook, organizer of birthday parties, shopper, baker, sewer, housewife; the daughter is mainly mother's helper — like mother, like daughter — cooking, shopping etc. If in one instance she's out of character hunting for squirrels, climbing trees or playing baseball, she is considered "a problem" and Daddy sits down with her; she ends up begging him to get her a new party-dress. The son on the other hand is more like father: David settles disputes between his two sisters, he earns money with his paper-route, leads the class in Science and helps the girls with their school problems; David at the early age of seven seems to demonstrate wisdom.

Consider the cruelty of all this. Little children proudly learning to recognize the written word and all the while their minds are being sabotaged. This sexism in children's readers is a reflection of our sexist society. If we wish to destroy sexism, we must stop using the tools that perpetuate it.

The Royal Commission Report on the Status of Women in Canada lists appropriate recommendations under the section entitled *Education,* particularly *Education and Stereotypes,* items 42-57. In this section, the socialization of children by parents as well as by the formal educational system is discussed and found to be lacking. "We urge Canadian parents to be especially sensitive to the individuality and aptitudes of both girls and boys." About the sex-typing in text books, the Commission says:

> Although such influences may seem insignificant to an adult reader, it is important to remember that the readers are children and that they learn through models whom to imitate.

The Class (Women in Modern Society, Loyola, 1971/72) wrote to several Canadian publishers, and 50% of those who answered assured us that they were making efforts to eliminate sexism. However, one firm stated:

> We have run into the same kind of frustration that your students encountered in their research. However, our frustrations are multiplied because of numerous factors that must be considered in selecting materials. Some of these factors relate to: sex, ethnic backgrounds, age, interest and appropriateness of topics, level of reading difficulty, inclusion of varied occupations and geographical backgrounds, literary quality, content to promote development of varied reading skills, exclusion of vulgar and profane language, content to promote wholesome life values and positive, creative attitudes about themselves and others, and so on. It should now be clearly evident that finding materials to meet all these requirements is very difficult. The fact that the members of the public body have varying opinions, standards, and needs makes our task doubly difficult. However, our materials have always

presented individuals and groups in situations that reflect a sense of fairness and respect.

Two publishers have in the meantime sent us their most recent basal readers and we note *some* improvement. The question is, of course, when the various school boards will introduce better material. To achieve this, parents and teachers will have to be more critical. May we ask you to look at the books your children use in school and preschool classes? And to voice your opinions as strongly as possible?

The above essay is a collective critique composed of excerpts from students' criticisms of children's literature.

CHORALLY SEXIST

by

Sylvia Green

Harmonic Husband Hunting

Mother, I want a husband.
"Who shall it be, my dearest child?
Shall it be a Frenchman?"
No, Mother, no.
A Frenchman, he would never do,
I understand no parlez-vous.
My greatest joy is the local farmer boy.

* * *

High, Betty Martin, tip toe, tip toe,
High, Betty Martin, tip toe fine.
Never found a boy to suit her fancy,
Never found a boy to suit her mind.

* * *

There was a young lady,
Or so I've heard tell,
Who wanted to marry,
To marry quite well.

He had to be perfect,
The man she would get.
So, unless I'm mistaken,
She's waiting there yet!

* * *

Mary Anne, Mary Anne, when will you wed?
My Mary Anne, Mary Anne, when will you wed?
When I'm a lady and when he's a man.
Hop-sa-sa, fa-la-la, my Mary Anne.

* * *

Domestic Symphony

How many buttons are missing today?
Nobody knows but mother.
How many playthings are strewn in her way?
Nobody knows but mother.

How many muddy shoes all in a row?
Nobody knows but mother.
How many stockings to darn, do you know?
Nobody knows but mother.

How many lunches for Tommy and Sam?
Nobody knows but mother.
Cookies and apples and blackberry jam?
Nobody knows but mother.

* * *

Mother Goose

Mother rocks her baby dear, Lullaby, my baby;
Heav'nly angels guard thee here, Lullaby, my baby;
Tiny shoes and coat of gold. Keep my darling from the cold;
Lullaby, my baby.

* * *

Oh My Beloved Daddy

We put more coal on the big red fire,
And while we are waiting for dinner to cook,
Our father comes and tells us about
A story that he has read in a book.

And when we are sitting very still,
He sings us a song or tells a piece,
He sings, "Dan Tucker Went to Town,"
Or tells us about the golden fleece.

* * *

Beauty Itself

That girl with the flaming red hair — *clap, clap,*
That girl with the saucy blue eyes — *clap, clap,*
Bewitching beyond compare — *clap, clap,*
Oh, she is the one that I prize — *clap, clap.*

* * *

Her brow is like the snowdrift,
Her neck is like the swan,
Her face, it is the fairest,
That ever the sun shone on.

* * *

She's fair like a rose,
Like a lamb she is meek,
And she never was known to put paint on her cheek,
In the most graceful curls
Hangs her ravenblack hair,
And she never requires perfumery there.

* * *

Romance on a Theme of Lies

Oh, I met a hand-some prince in my wooden shoes,
Oh, I met a hand-some prince in my wooden shoes,
Now the hand-some prince he loves me in my wooden shoes,
Tra la, la, la, la, la, in my wooden shoes.

* * *

On Richmond Hill there lives a lass,
More bright than Mayday morn,
Whose charms all other maids surpass,
A rose without a thorn.

* * *

I'd like to make that gal my wife,
Gal my wife, gal my wife,
Then I'd be happy all my life,
If I had her by me.

* * *

Radiant with love the maid awakes;
High on his stead his bride he takes;
Safe from enchantment they fly.
All now rejoice,
Birds find a voice,
Flames from the hearth
Leap up toward the sky.

* * *

Woman Is Passivity

The evening had gathered around her
On a branch of the green lemon tree.
And the breezes were whispering to her,
Little bird sing your sweet melody,
Oh yes, oh no, when will my love come to me?

* * *

She sat by her window,
Both early and late.
And there she would wait,
And would wait, and would wait!

She sat there all smiles; and
She sat there all tears;
She waited for days;
And she waited for years.

* * *

Once was a maid in forest deep
Lay for a hundred years asleep;

34

Slumber no sound ever could break;
All things alive,
Bees in the hive,
Fires on the hearth,
Could not stay awake.

Came there a Prince with banners gay,
Riding along the forest way,
Spies he the maid in the brake
Springs from his steed,
Sees Beauty's need
Kneels over the maid to kiss her awake.

* * *

But Man Is Activity

Where the pools are bright and deep,
Where the gray trout lies asleep;
Up the river and o'er the sea,
That's the way for Billy and me.

* * *

We climb the trees and go on hikes,
And all grow strong and brown,
Our friends will hardly know us
When we go back to town.

We do not miss the telephone,
The movies, or the cars,
When we can fish and hike all day,
And sleep beneath the stars.

* * *

Tom, Tom, the piper's son,
Stole a pig, and away he run;
The pig got loose and stole a goose,
And Tom got put in the calaboose.

* * *

Oh, the oil station man is our friend, friend, friend.
Our bicycles tires he'll mend, mend, mend.
He puts on a patch and sizz, sizz, sizz,
He blows up our tires and away we whizz.

* * *

Not long after spending too much time, money, and energy obtaining my music supervisor's degree, I couldn't help but feel there must be a better way of exposing children to music than the one proposed in the basal music textbooks. Singing from them was a bore, and the children hated it. I consequently decided to free myself from these texts, to experiment with other ways of making music a joy for children, and to do away with what I would call Basal Brainwashing.

In addition to being dull and non-creative, the songs in the textbooks are full of sexist material, as are the textbooks used in other subjects. Under such influences — and there are many — little girls especially rarely develop their innate creative potential, and as a result many grow to be like the women depicted in our children's songs.

First we have *Harmonic Husband Hunting*: in many of the songs, such as "Mother, I want a Husband," girls are concerned with finding a man and getting married. Marriage in fact seems to be the major goal of women in all the eleven books used for this study.

If "Betty Martin" is not preoccupied with finding her love, the neighbours certainly are. As in the case of the "Young Lady," there is an underlying tone of social disgrace in remaining single.

The second act of our musical drama is called *Domestic Symphony*:

Buttons, lunches, blackberry jam,
Washing, starching, hanging out;
Baking cakes,
sewing seams,
Rock-a-by, hush —
The baby wakes.

The above description of mother's domestic role is a composite picture of the songs about mothers.

By singing these songs and looking at the accompanying pictures, little girls soon come to believe that this too will be their lot in life after they have found a husband. And they are led to believe it is fun.

While Mother is *Mother Goose* — rearing the children, teaching them manners, putting baby to bed, and always aware of where the children are, Father brings the fine things of life. Of course, he can do this only when he is not too busy in the outside world. When he has the time, he will read to the children and he will

36

also bring home candy, a kitten, or maybe a puppy-dog. In any case, not one of the books depicts Father as taking part in *Mother Goose* activities. But he remains *Oh My Beloved Daddy*, a busy and knowledgeable hero.

The ideal woman, children learn while singing these songs, is *Beauty Itself*. A strange beauty, an unattainable beauty, with a brow like a snowdrift, a neck like the swan's, hands as white as snow, etc. etc. On the whole, a superhuman beauty, as fair as a rose, which can only lead to the frustration of females who are being taught to emulate these fictitious goddesses.

Realizing but not accepting their own imperfections, most women today go to great pains and expense attempting artificially to make themselves beautiful as the phoney archetypes portrayed in these songs. I feel that a "snowdrift-shaped" brow and a neck "like the swan" *dehumanize woman.*

If *Beauty Itself* is harmful, *Romance On A Theme Of Lies* represents real danger. The false, sugary picture of love and courtship makes children believe that this is the way it actually happens. When they come of age, they are disillusioned by the realization that it is not quite as easy as conveyed in childhood songs.

Not many men really would die for "The Lass of Richmond Hill", or any other for that matter. And although this neat, sweet lass doesn't exist, women foolishly try to emulate her. Men are frustrated because as boys they were taught that she lives at Richmond Hill; yet when they go there, they find out it is a lie.

Even if a girl doesn't believe that by wearing "Wooden Shoes" she will meet a handsome prince, sudden interest in clothes and simultaneous interest in boys is not purely coincidental! If you don the right clothes, you will meet your dream-boy.

Although most girls would agree that *Sleeping Beauty* is realistically impossible, they do believe in bliss forever after. As it turns out, once a girl marries, the opposite is more often true — she goes into a deep sleep, fusing with the personality of her husband, giving up her own individuality.

It is indeed sad that the texts from which these songs have been taken are still 'standard equipment' in Canadian school music programs.

It is hoped that studies like this one will alert educators to the reality of sexual typing which they (consciously or unconsciously) are promoting by using these texts.

I have no regrets now that I have cut up my music books to illustrate my term paper. Each has been suffering from a terrible disease. The remains shall be laid to rest in the dust of the basement locker.

The songs in this study have been taken from the following texts:
Singing On Our Way (Ginn)
Songtime 3 (Holt, Rinehart, and Winston)
Singing and Rhyming (Ginn)
Singing Every Day (Ginn)
The New High Road of Song 4 (Gage)
The New High Road of Song 5 (Gage)
Songs For Today, Volume Six (Waterloo)
High Road of Song Intermediate 1 (Gage)
High Road of Song Intermediate 2 (Gage)
Singing Junior (Ginn)
Singing Teen-agers (Ginn)

THE BECOMING OF CAROLINE[1]

by

Margaret Gillett

In the field of Education, we talk a lot about individual differences — how teachers should recognize them, how the curriculum should be organized around them, how the schools should foster them. Yet, I am inclined to think this is one of the greatest con games in contemporary education. We still do not think in terms of individuals; we really worry about categories. We acknowledge that the quest for individual identity is one of the all-important concerns of education but — perhaps it's the pressure of mass age numbers — we are hung up on roles. Socially defined roles certainly can engender a sense of security, they may even be short-cuts to identity; but they are pre-packaged, not custom-made;

38

they may be convenient, but they are not always apt; they tell you what you're supposed to do, not who you are. Just last week, I heard of a homely, but very telling, example of this.

A colleague of mine has a three-year-old daughter, Caroline. She recently had her hair cut short and her father, who perhaps is not quite up-to-date with boys' hairdos, teased her and said, "Caroline's a boy, Caroline's a boy!" "I'm not," cried Caroline in confusion and distress, "I'm a girl." Caroline likes to go shopping. She decided to go by herself and, being a practical child, she took along most of the things in her mother's jewelry box, including the housekeeping money. Hours later, her frantic mother located her at the police station (with only $12 left). The police had picked her up near the highway but, though she knows her name and address very well, she wouldn't give them to the police. All she would say was, "I'm a girl. I'm a girl."

The question is, how will she become Caroline? There are enormous pressures for her to accept and to play a role — the role of girl as our society has defined it.

The influences start very subtly and very early. In infancy, Caroline was put in pink, not blue, baby clothes. Those innocent pink booties could become bonds of expectation and perhaps they are really only milder forms of the classic Chinese footbinding which physically, as well as psychologically, defined the role girls would play.

As Caroline emerged from infancy, she was still allowed to play with cuddly toys and was permitted to cry — not so her brother. She has learned some winning, "girlish" ways — she follows her mother around the house with a duster and a tiny mop, she empties her father's ashtrays, she's encouraged to be clean and tidy, while her brother is playing ball outside in the mud.

Next year, she'll go to kindergarten and soon she'll learn to read. In children's books, she'll find plenty of reinforcement for the role for which she is being programmed. She will probably encounter as many girls as boys in the stories she reads. For the most part they will be girls with dolls, girls with kittens, girls who help with the new baby just like a little mommy. There will be some, but few, dynamic girls and non-domesticated women. According to a recent "women's" magazine article on children's books, most of the mothers portrayed will be vapid and passive, most of them serving as cooks, laundresses, and cleaning women. I hope Caroline will not read a blatant apology for the status quo by a Whitney Darrow called *I'm Glad I'm a Boy! I'm Glad I'm a Girl!* It says fearlessly, "Boys have trucks." "Girls have dolls." "Boys are doctors." "Girls are nurses." "Boys fix things." "Girls need things fixed." "Girls can cook." "Boys invent things." "Girls use what boys invent." Caroline will probably not be able to escape the formula story of the tomboy who, at the end of the book, concedes that her mother was right, that dresses can be pretty, and gives up "boyish" activities in favor of her traditional role of helper and tea-pourer.

What is called "sexism in children's literature" is at last rousing serious concern and has recently been the subject of papers in popular magazines and learned journals as well as at Children's Book Week conferences. This exposure of the subtle indoctrination is welcome, but I think it should be pointed out that the issue is not really one of sex — or sexism — but it's a matter of gender. This distinction really ought to be preserved throughout the entire debate on Women's Lib.

But to return to Caroline — as she goes up through the school system, even though she attends co-ed schools, she will find that there are still "girl's" subjects and "boy's" subjects and that teachers and guidance people will try to channel her into appropriate "girl's" programs. She may take an interest in sports, but in her highschool years she will learn that it may be all right to play well but not *too* well if she is to conform to the social mores and dating patterns. Otherwise, she may find that she has no boyfriends and may later have an experience like the one I had here in Troy while I was at Russell Sage. I used to play tennis on the public courts in the park at the top of the hill. One day I played with a young man who happened to be a Negro and, perhaps, I beat him. At the end he said, "You play well — for a woman." His condescension was unconscious and I didn't have the heart to reply, "You play well for a Negro." It is just assumed, deep down, that women are always inferior — and we're supposed to accept it. Women's role, in sports especially, is to stop doing and become spectators or, as the swinging hockey star of the Boston Bruins, Derek Sanderson, said, "Girls are just part of the equipment."

Anyway, when Caroline gets to college, she may be able to take a course in Women's Studies and get a systematic analysis of all this. She may be amazed to discover that John Stuart Mill's great book, *The Subjection of Women,* was written as long ago as 1869 and she might also be surprised to discover that a man, Ashley Montagu, wrote a book on *The Natural Superiority of Women.* She'll find other revelations in works like Mary Beard's

40

Women as Force in History, Caroline Bird's *Born Female,* Simone de Beauvoir's *The Second Sex,* and Kate Millett's *Sexual Politics.* She may get fired up or furious with the essays now pouring out of the Women's Lib. movement — Robin Morgan's *The Sisterhood is Powerful,* for example, and she may be lucky enough to get hold of the best-selling Canadian publication, *Royal Commission Report on the Status of Women.* She may simply encounter this question in her general reading. Perhaps she'll come across Meredith's statement, "Woman is the last thing to be civilized by man" (1859); or she'll see Ibsen's *Doll's House;* or laugh at Thurber's perennial "battle of the sexes;" or read Virginia Woolf's *A Room of One's Own.* She may or may not be amused by Dr. Johnson's intended witticism about the educated woman and the performing dog — it's not a question of how well they do it, it's against nature and a miracle that they do it at all!

But our Caroline is more likely to be reading Marshall McLuhan than Dr. Johnson. She will find that he claims in the *Gutenberg Galaxy* that by 1929 women had been homogenized by the movies and photo advertising, reduced to uniformity and repeatability. In *The Mechanical Bride,* she will read how "the images of advertisements and movies presented a mechanized image for women. Although her skirts were shortened, the woman of the thirties and forties pulled herself *in* with corsets and *up* with bras; glamor photos were taken on tiptoe, emphasizing the rigidity of the mechanical pull on the leg; the individual piece of anatomy — a leg with a stocking, a bust with a bra — were illustrated as fragments or replaceable parts. Finally, in the forties, the drum majorette appeared — An adolescent love notice, a junior chorus girl in cavalry officer attire . . . instructed in the art of symbolic flagellation.''

Caroline may scoff at these generalities and want to go on with her education and her career. The idea of her becoming a physician, for example, is not impossible and she won't have to fight the strenuous battles of a hundred years ago. Maria Montessori, Italy's first woman doctor and later famous educator, had to argue her way into medical school, had to be escorted by a chaperone and, since it was not decorous for a young woman to work on cadavers with men, she had to practice her anatomy alone at night. Caroline won't have that, but she may have quotas to contend with and subtle discriminations that manage to keep the number of female physicians in the U.S. at about 6% of the total (in contrast to 85% in the U.S.S.R.). If she decides

41

to take up another career, she will also encounter prejudice. This is one reason why Claire Kirkland-Casgrain, the only woman in the Quebec National Assembly, has said that women in politics are "as rare as whooping cranes." And even here in the U.S. you don't have many, though two new ones were elected to the present Congress. There was once a woman mayor of Ottawa, Canada's capital. She was Charlotte Whitton and she pointed out that, for a woman to succeed in business or politics, she had to be at least twice as good as a man and, she added, "Luckily, this isn't difficult!" There was also once a woman in the Canadian cabinet, Judy LaMarsh. She wrote in her memoirs that she was always something of a second class citizen, not in the mainstream, partly because so many of the important decisions were made in a place from which she was banned, the executive washroom.

But Caroline might decide to go in for teaching, traditionally a woman's job. If she does, she will most likely get equal pay, but she will find that the path to promotion is narrow, that relatively few high schools have women principals and that a decreasing number of elementary schools have women at the head. If she teaches at the college level she will discover that, as late as 1970, women were discriminated against in terms of hiring, promotion, salary, and administrative appointments. A recent study at McGill, my university, shows unhappily that this is true there — though I myself cannot complain.

Meanwhile, she will have had the privileges of citizenship — including the right to vote, accorded to women in America after World War I, not until 1940 in the Province of Quebec, and in Switzerland in 1971. But she has long had the privilege of paying equal taxes. Though it is unlikely that she got equal tax breaks. There are no arrangements for a deductible wife for women, even though it has clearly been recognized that every professional woman needs a wife.

As Caroline grows older, she will have to cope with questions of pension plan benefits, annuities and insurance policies, special medical deductions and retirement schemes. All this complexity might make her sympathize with the elderly widow from Vancouver who complained that computing the estate taxes gave her so much trouble that she was almost sorry her husband had died. And perhaps this is where, finally, the bonus is. If Caroline has played her role properly, she will have been protected from the hurly-burly of the world and she will inherit all the money her husband grew ulcers to make. You really can't wonder that nowadays Men's Liberation groups are beginning to form. They'll

42

be needed as long as the social expectations are so unfair; as long as men are forced into typically aggressive and competitive roles which they, as individuals, may not want to play; and as long as the situation can be exploited by wily women.

It is perfectly obvious that until people, all people, are permitted to grow up and define their identities in their own terms — not as adjuncts to someone else nor just as patterns in the social mosaic — no one will really be free. And it will only be when we truly allow for individual differences and worry less about roles that our heroine will stop being a girl and will become Caroline. I hope she makes it.

1. Address given at the Cap and Gown Convocation, Russell Sage College, Troy, N.Y., April 27, 1971. Reprinted from the *McGill Journal of Education*, Fall 1971, Vol. VI, No. 2.

Moving Day For an Old Woman:

Crowded in boxes, brooding with past,
wrinkled linens in regal embroidery,
yellowed doilies of filigreed memory,
dated the lot, but woven to last.

Restless she checked her possessions, numbered,
labeled, tied up and identified.
Restless she scurried, now unencumbered,
now feeling herself inventorized.

Thought chains, familiar, unraveling, caught her,
tears, beading against the enfeebled thread.
Should she succumb to become a collector,
or go on making doilies, instead?

inge packer

THE QUESTION OF THE LAW

No woman, idiot, lunatic, or criminal shall vote.

From the Election Act
of the Dominion of Canada

The stance of the law in regard to women is rich
in gallantry and paternalism.

Marvin Zuker, June Callwood
Canadian Women and the Law, 1971.

WOMEN AND THE LAW

by

Janet Kask

A male prostitute in Canada doesn't have the same legal problems as a female in the same trade because the Federal Criminal Code agrees with Webster's New Collegiate in assuming a prostitute is a "woman given to indiscriminate lewdness for hire."

There's nothing in the Code that describes or defines prostitution as illegal but it does impose a curfew on the female prostitute. If a known prostitute sitting in a downtown bar can't give "a good account of herself" she can be picked up for vagrancy and charged, fined or jailed. But the man who does business with her isn't committing an offence.

The double standard operates against men when it comes to other kinds of sexual offences in the Code. In the law women can't sexually assault or seduce men because it's generally assumed that they're the victims, not the authors, of sexual crimes.

There's still some housekeeping to be done to rid Canadian law of cobwebs of custom and morality that discriminate against both sexes, but in most cases against women. The Citizenship Act, for example, still treats the married woman as a second class citizen. When a Canadian male takes himself a foreign-born wife she can become a Canadian citizen after one year. But a Canadian female's foreign-born husband must wait five years for citizenship. The child born abroad of a Canadian father has the automatic right to Canadian citizenship, but the child of a Canadian woman, unless she's unmarried or divorced, hasn't.

"It's based on the patriarchal notion of society that citizenship rights are passed on through the man," says Montreal lawyer Dionysia Zerbisias.

Before 1947 a Canadian woman who married a non-Canadian lost her citizenship. If she let the matter lapse she still has to re-apply to the Secretary of State for citizenship.

There's no Canadian law stating that a woman must change her name to her husband's when she marries. But if she wants a passport she has to apply for a new one — under her husband's name. A married professional woman can keep her maiden name on her passport but her marital status and married name must be included too. On the passport of a child whose parents are married, only the father's signature will do.

The Immigration Act refers in various sections to "head of family": normally interpreted as the husband, points out Miss Zerbisias. Often a married woman will make application for admission to the country and on the basis of her qualifications could be admitted, but because she's a woman she's always admitted under her husband's qualifications.

"They [the immigration officials] don't seem to recognize the roles held by women today in assuming many of the financial responsibilities of the family. What I really object to is the fact that as far as I know, women are taxed on the same scale as males. If they aren't going to have equal rights, then they should be taxed on a preferential basis too."

Under the Immigration Act, if a woman's husband is deported she can be deported under the same order. This is based on the philosophy that a woman must follow her husband wherever he goes.

The same idea underlies the law regarding legal domicile. A married woman's domicile is that of her husband unless she seeks a divorce; or, in Quebec, if she's been granted a legal separation.

The Indian Act also discriminates against the married woman. The Indian woman who marries a non-Indian loses all her rights and privileges under the act. Her children lose theirs as well. But the man who marries a non-Indian confers the privileges on his wife and children. The federal government's 1969 statement on Indian policy said "To be an Indian is to be a man, with all a man's needs and abilities."

Jeannette Vivian Lavell, who had her name struck from the register of the Wikwemikonk Band in Ontario when she married a non-Indian, disagreed. She took her case to court on the grounds that the Indian Act wasn't in keeping with the guarantees of the Canadian Bill of Rights. If she wins the case in the Supreme Court where it is pending review now, it will be the first time that the Bill of Rights has been used to battle discrimination against women.

But the lawyers I talked to didn't think the Bill of Rights

was strong enough to combat every day discrimination such as job classification, unequal pay and landlords' prejudices. Most provinces have laws guaranteeing civil rights but in too many cases they're also considered too vague.

"Any area of obvious provable discrimination should be made a serious offence with strong penalties attached," says lawyer Lilian Reinblatt. "But most present legislation doesn't have enough gut in it. We need good strong laws with plenty of teeth in them to make them work."

She cited the Ontario Women's Equal Employment Opportunities Act passed in 1970 as an example of what Quebec needs to protect women against discriminatory practices, but she claimed that the act was designed to place responsibility for the protection of women's employment rights in the hands of the Women's Bureau of the Department of Labor. Mrs. Reinblatt believes this is an inadequate instrument for a commission safe-guarding human rights. She agrees with the recommendation of the Royal Commission's Report on the Status of Women that human rights commissions with wide powers designed for the protection of all Canadians be set up at federal and provincial levels. The Quebec Civil Liberties Union has recently been pressing for this in Quebec.

Job classification is a major issue of contention in women's pursuit for equal rights. Want-ads in most Canadian newspapers still have separate sections for males and females in their "help wanted" columns. The Girl Friday in the female column may carry out the same duties as the Junior Executive in the male section but she's paid much less. Women often find themselves in jobs where they're doing the same work as men, but their job is called something else. Male-female distinctions are even written into union contracts and tacitly agreed upon by employers and employees. In a few provinces with strong anti-discrimination legislation, companies and unions are now being reported and in some cases taken to court.

Lawyer Louise MacKay believes that while the law discriminates, society is the real culprit. While a lot of legislation has been brought up to date within the last few years to combat discrimination based on sex there's still a dearth of women in high places. In the legal profession women are submitted to as much discrimination as women in other fields. Women lawyers, she pointed out, don't become senior partners in law firms. They remain employees or junior partners whatever their abilities. While there are 84 women lawyers registered with the Montreal Bar Association, only one was named a Superior Court judge. There are no female judges in Appeal, Provincial, Sessions or Municipal courts. There are a few in Social Welfare courts because that's considered a "woman's" field of interest.

Only last June a law was passed by Quebec's National Assembly allowing women to serve on juries. But the law is written in such a way that women, unlike most men, can refuse to sit on juries. Quebec's Justice Minister Jerôme Choquette explained at the time (1971) that women were "a different class of people before the law," because of domestic and "health" reasons. The latter was meant to cover pregnancy and menstruation. The jury law doesn't represent any change from the sexist mentality that prevailed before it was passed.

A single woman still has more de facto equality than her married sister. The married woman in Quebec, who not too many years ago was described in the province's civil code as "incapable" along with "minors, interdicted persons and insane or temporarily deranged persons," now has complete legal freedom to run her own affairs. But many business establishments continue to assume she's financially dependent on her husband and women who apply for credit cards and buy property find they're still being asked for a husband's signature.

One lawyer pointed out that some medical insurance plans discriminate against the married woman. There are plans where a woman can't declare her husband and children as dependent participants, but a man in the same situation can declare his wife and children as his dependents. "There's no legal justification for it."

The law still doesn't recognize the housewife (or househusband) as part of the labor force. (A West German court recently estimated a housewife's labor was worth $10,000 a year.) They aren't entitled to pensions under the Canada Pension Plan or the Quebec Pension Plan.

Married women (or men) who choose to work in the home as home-makers are the only employees in contemporary western society who receive no salaries for their labor. They are dependent on the good will of the spouse who brings in the salary.

With the passing of Bill 10 in 1969, Quebec's official matrimonial regime called Partnership of Acquests became law and was hailed by some as the most advanced matrimonial system in North America. Under the regime when a marriage dissolves by death or separation, all financial earnings and property acquired by both spouses during the marriage are split in half. The Quebec Bar Association and the Civil Liberties Union said this system
50

made marriage too difficult to dissolve because of the complications arising from dividing property.

Many Quebec couples still opt for the separation of property system in which a financial agreement is defined in a marriage contract drawn up by a notary. When the marriage is dissolved by divorce, gifts promised in the contract can be claimed by court action but alimony may be ruled in favor of either spouse. Separation of property may be more favorable to a woman than Partnership of Acquests if her husband dies and she's entitled to a large sum in the contract. But if he dies a millionaire and the contract says she's entitled to $15,000, she's better off under the Acquests system. Her husband is still free to leave the remaining amount to whomever he chooses.

Grounds for divorce have been broadened since 1968 changes in the Divorce Act, but there's still no divorce by mutual consent as there is in several other countries where divorce has been liberalized. In divorce proceedings it's always assumed that there's a guilty and an innocent party even though in most cases both parties contribute to marriage breakdown. And divorce in Canada is still expensive — between $500-$800.

"Law is the most conservative of our institutions," said Mrs. Reinblatt. "We just catch up and change laws when the public demand is so terrific that we have to. We must encourage people to enter the legal profession who will use their knowledge and experience to keep our laws up to date with the constantly changing needs of a rapidly evolving society."

LABOUR LEGISLATION IN QUEBEC AND ONTARIO

by

Lilian Reinblatt

ARTICLE 174 of The Civil Code of the Province of Quebec: *A husband owes protection to his wife: a wife obedience to her husband.*

This provision of our Civil Code existed as recently as 1964, having its origins in early French Law and the Napoleonic Code. It was removed by the well known enacted Provincial legislation 'Bill 16' which began to establish equal legal status, capacity and rights for the married woman in the Province of Quebec. Thus finally we have eliminated in North American society the last vestiges of the mediaeval and feudal concept of obedience which married women owed to their husbands.

Today the married woman in Quebec finally has achieved equal legal status and capacity, with the equal rights and obligations of her husband in Quebec society. However equal legal status and capacity does not automatically ensure equal pay for equal work, equality of opportunity in the labour force, or lack of discrimination in employment. Only legislation can give women equal rights while she is working. More difficult, however, is legislation to guarantee equal opportunity and equal rights to a job.

One of the principles of the United Nations, which was born in 1945, was its concern for human rights and fundamental freedoms, and Canada, being a charter member was committed to the principle of the rights of women to employment with equal pay, with the adoption in 1948 of the Universal Declaration of Human Rights. Article 23 of the Declaration proclaims that:

> 1. Everyone has the right to work, to free choice of employment, to just and favourable conditions of work and to protection against unemployment.

2. Everyone, without discrimination, has the right to equal pay for equal work.

In 1967, the United Nation's General Assembly unanimously adopted the Declaration on the Elimination of Discrimination of Women. Article 10-1 of this Declaration states that women have:

a) the right, without discrimination on grounds of marital status or any other grounds, to receive vocational training, to work, to free choice of professional and vocational advancement: and

b) the right to equal remuneration with men and to equality of treatment in respect of work of equal value.

Canada, too, ratified the Convention concerning Discrimination in Respect of Employment and Occupation: Convention 111 of the International Labour Organization. In doing so, Canada agreed to ''undertake to declare and pursue a national policy designed to promote, by methods appropriate to national conditions and practice, equality of opportunity and treatment in respect of employment and occupation with a view to eliminating any discrimination in respect thereof.''

Since labour legislation falls within the jurisdiction of the provinces under the British North America Act, Canada, has not, due to provincial differences and conflicting opinion, ratified the International Labour Organization convention concerning equal remuneration for men and women workers for work of equal value (convention 100.) The Royal Commission Report on the Status of Women recommended the ratification of that convention.

There exists wide acceptance — international, federal and provincial — of the principle of 'equal pay for equal work.' Most provinces and the federal government have adopted, and implemented in various forms, legislation which covers the principle of equal pay and anti-discrimination legislation. In 1956, the federal government passed anti-discrimination legislation, called the Female Employees Equal Pay Act, applicable to employer and employees engaged in works, undertakings and businesses under federal jurisdiction and to federal Crown Corporations. However, as recently as 1968, there were still people who apparently thought there should be different rates of pay for women and men. In rendering a decision regarding the claim of a policewoman for equal pay with policemen in 1968, a judge of the Ontario High Court stated ''she is not being discriminated against by the fact that she receives a different wage, different from male constables, for the fact of difference is in accord with every rule of economics, civilization, family life and common sense."[1]

Quebec legislation makes no particular reference to the subject of equal pay, but does prohibit sex discrimination in employment (the Discrimination in Employment Act, 1964). The laws are not as effective as one would wish because many exceptions to the law are allowed, penalties are far too lenient to be effective, and there is neither protection of employment, nor provision for restitution of losses. In addition, the action must be initiated by the aggrieved person.

Ontario took the lead with the passage in 1951 of the Female Employees Fair Remuneration Act, which was subsequently replaced by other legislation. The Women's Equal Employment Opportunity Act or an Act to Prevent Discrimination in Employment because of Sex or Marital Status was assented to in Ontario, in June, 1970. Subsequent amendments and regulations have contributed to the many improvements and this legislation has been strengthened and transferred to the Ontario Human Rights Code, by the Ontario Human Rights Code Amendment Act, effective June 29, 1972. The Act is administered by a Human Rights Commission. The preamble of the Ontario Human Rights Code reads in part as follows:

> Whereas recognition of the inherent dignity and the equal and inalienable rights of all members of the human family is the foundation of freedom, justice and peace in the world and is in accord with the Universal Declaration of Human Rights as proclaimed by the United Nations;
>
> And whereas it is public policy in Ontario that every person is free and equal in dignity and rights without regard to race, creed, colour, sex, marital status, nationality, ancestry or place of origin;
>
> And whereas these principles have been confirmed in Ontario by a number of enactments of the Legislature.

Previously, the Human Rights Code provided protection against discrimination in employment only on the grounds of race, creed, color, nationality or place of origin. Sex and marital status have also been added to the prohibitions in *non-employment* situations which include housing accommodation, notices, signs and access to public places.

Thus not only does the Human Rights Code provide for legislation against discrimination in employment practices, which include referrals, recruitment, dismissals, training, promotion, transfers, etc, but in addition, the former provisions in the Code dealing with discriminatory advertising now includes an amendment prohibiting publishers from classifying, either directly or indirectly discriminatory job advertisements. This means that Help-Wanted columns segregated according to sex will no longer be permitted. The prohibition of discrimination in trade union membership is extended to self-governing professions and covers discrimination on the basis of sex, marital status and age.

Procedural provisions have been added and strengthened to augment the Commission's effectiveness. These measures enable the Human Rights Commission to initiate an enquiry where there are reasons to believe that the Human Rights Code has been contravened and increase maximum fines for non-compliance to $1,000.00 for individuals and up to $5,000.00 for Corporations.

Moreover, the Ontario government has recently appointed an Interministerial Committee on the Status of Women Report to review those recommendations of the Royal Commission on the Status of Women that come under provincial jurisdiction. This, unfortunately, does not exist in the Province of Quebec. Nor, even more unfortunately, does a Human Rights Code, nor a Human Rights Commission.

With the example of the recent Ontario legislation and amendments and Recommendation No. 8 of the Royal Commission Report on the Status of Women[2]. It becomes acutely obvious that our present labour legislation with regard to the interests of women, needs immediate revision and updating.

---

1. Beckett V. City of Sault Ste-Marie Police Commissioners et al. 67 Dominion Law Reports: 2nd ed. 1968, p. 294.
2. We recommend that the federal Female Employees Equal Pay Act, the Federal Fair Wages and Hours of Work Regulations and Equal Pay Legislation of Provinces and Territories require that a) the concept of skill, effort and responsibility be used as objective factors in determining what is equal work, with the understanding that pay rates thus established will be subject to such factors as seniority provisions; b) an employee who feels aggrieved as a result of an alleged violation of the relevant legislation, or a party acting on her behalf, be able to refer the grievance to the agency designated for that purpose by the government administering the legislation; c) the onus of investigating violations of the legislation be placed in the hands of the agency administering the equal pay legislation which will be free to investigate, whether or not complaints have been laid; d) to the extent possible, the anonymity of the complainant be maintained; e) provision be made for authority to render a decision on whether or not the terms of the legislation have been violated,

to specify action to be taken and to prosecute if the orders are not followed; *f)* where someone has presented the aggrieved employee's case on her behalf and the aggrieved employee is unsatisfied with the decision, she have the opportunity to present her case herself to the person or persons rendering the decision who may change the decision; *g)* the employee's employment status be in no way adversely affected by the application of the law to her case; *h)* where the law has been violated, the employee be compensated for any losses in pay, vacation and other fringe benefits; *i)* unions and employee organizations, as well as employers and employer organizations, be subject to this law; *j)* the penalties be sufficiently heavy to be an effective deterrent; and *k)* the legislation specify that it is applicable to part-time as well as to full-time workers.

THE QUESTION OF MARRIAGE

This dependence of the wife upon her husband causes her to be classed in society among those persons who are considered incapable.

Marie Gérin-Lajoie, 1902

The world has taunted women into marrying.

Nellie McClung, 1916

the ball-less man, sat in the bus, in his best suit
looking as
if every
nice-looking girl
would desire him,
awfully,
for her husband.

mary melfi, 1971

SCATTERED THOUGHTS ON MARRIAGE

by

Kathy Gower

Since entering into the institution of marriage — voluntarily — over two years ago, my husband and I have experienced the nagging feeling of being cheated. Not by one another, but by some indefinable quality that the institution itself had taken from — or given to — our relationship. An entire gamut of sexual, financial and domestic obligations and expectations were created by that legal bond, unconscious expectations that we fell in line with because, in essence, we were, as a married couple, viewed differently by friends, relatives, and strangers. For both, the resultant feeling was entrapment. After some investigation, we discovered the source was in neither of us, but in the institution. And the logical conclusion resulting from that realization was that the institution of marriage may be obsolete.

I felt the need to further investigate this entire question of marriage. How did it originate, had it always been the same, why do we continue to choose it as a way of life, and just what is marriage anyway?

Unfortunately, I have not found any clear cut answers to those questions. I discovered that 'scientific' theories on the origins of marriage, for example, are culturally biased; they accept monogamous marriage as the highest form of man-woman relationship possible. It is seen as the basis of the family, and the family is viewed as the basis of society. Research has been in the direction of helping men and women adjust to this all-important institution; seldom is the question raised of why so much adjustment seems to be necessary. Researchers have assumed that the natural state of mankind is this blatantly demoralizing institution where work is assigned according to sex. They have not helped me reconstruct the position of women in marriage through the ages as much

I would have liked; their effect was to support the present situation and I therefore made little headway with any one theory of the evolution of marriage.

A look at the present condition of marital relations seemed in order. An appropriate starting point is revealed in a sociological definition of marriage. "Marriage is a formal and durable sexual union of one or more men and one or more women, which is conducted within a set of designated rights and duties ... marriage requires that husband and wife fulfill certain rights and duties they expect of each other in their roles."[1] (Note: other definitions define marriage as such a union between one man and one woman only).

Simply put, the husband expects sex and sons, the wife security and sustenance. Our college manual (I even took a course on marriage), also lists more high-sounding motivations for marriage; companionship, emotional reassurance, emotional interdependence, freedom of communication and activity, and physical sexual fulfillment.[2] Of course, there is no discussion of why these "mature needs" can be met only in marriage, as our society expects, or how someone can be mature if he/she depends on another person for emotional reassurance. But ignoring that for the moment, the fact that middle-class North Americans search for a "meaningful interpersonal relationship in marriage should not obscure the fact that they often possess personality patterns and motivations that impose obstacles to the achievement of their marital goals ... the impersonality of life in our society ... imposes serious limitation on the person's ability to appreciate warm and meaningful human associations. Thus, in spite of a desire to find a meaningful relationship, husband and wife reared in an impersonal milieu tend to carry in to their home the values that govern their lives on the outside."[3]

Here we see that the authors attribute failure to attain a partnership that contributes to the intellectual and emotional growth of the individuals involved to general social ills. In part this is justifiable, but they overlook an explanation that they themselves point out: research on marriage prediction suggests that conservative and conventional people succeed best in marriage, because "marriage and the family are by nature conservative institutions."[4] This conservatism includes acceptance of sex-defined roles as well as lack of premarital sex, the male's choice of an occupation with social control, middle-class economic patterns of spending and saving and investing. So success in marriage is dependent on the traditional family structure of patriarchial authoritarianism.

This type of family includes these values: the authoritarian has a strong psychological need to be right; family control is based on irrational authority; the family is an association of unequals; and individual family members are treated as commodities. What the authors see as the emergent form of marriage, democratic individualism, expounds the values that family control is based on rational authority, that authority is associated with the desire to be right, that the family is an association of equals, and that family members are treated as ends in themselves.[5] So if conservative people succeed best in marriage, democratic individualism within that institution seems doomed to failure; the institution of marriage is not democratic.

Another study comments on this emergent form of marriage, and points out a situation inherent in marriage that certainly contributes to a large number of marital failures: "The democratic idea was to place the seat of authority in the family group itself, by distributing the power among all the members. In theory this was an excellent idea. But evidence is accumulating that in practice it will not work, because differentiation of roles is essential to good family functioning. All cannot be treated as equals, because in fact *they are not so.* A man and a woman may be equal as persons in society. But as husband and wife, acting out their masculine and feminine roles in marriage, they are different and complementary; the concept of equality is meaningless here."[6] So, as long as marriage is a legal contract set up to perpetuate the family — "the foundation stone of human society,"[7] men and women cannot be treated as equals. Equality disrupts the family. And since the family is looked upon as essential to civilization and since marriage is considered the basic adult human relationship, such studies as the one by David and Vera Mace cannot attack that inequality even though it sees it: it is committed to preserving it because it accepts the necessity of the family.

So instead of supporting woman in her attempt to escape this inherent inequality, scientists blame her wish to share authority for upsetting family relations. It appears that marital problems could be held at a controllable level if woman could only accept her traditional role. Democratic individualism, by undermining the authority of the man in the family "is not only damaging him, but hurting everyone else as well. The wife cannot function in her feminine role if her husband's masculine role is taken from him. The family group cannot function as a family if its natural head is dethroned ... if the husband can no longer play his part as leader and initiator, the wife is paralyzed in her responsive function,''[8] and is forced to wear the pants or become a hostile and demasculinizing female.

Thus they explain away the bewildered, restless, anxious demeanor of today's Western women. It is obvious that the authors consider it best for the family if the husband and wife accept their traditional roles, unequal though they may be. With such vested interest supporting marriage, it is no wonder that couples attempting to make their relationship an equal one have such difficulty. But it is strange to see that authors who consider the family as society's "foundation stone" believe a man and a women may be equal outside of marriage. Certainly they must realize their status in this basic institution has a tremendous effect on that society.

To David and Vera Mace, the wife appears victimized by this breakdown of authority because she cannot fulfill her natural role. "The mother should fill the role of best-liked person in the family. She should become the member who supports the weak, encourages the crestfallen, and holds the family together as a group.''[8] When the father doesn't assume his role of authority, she is caught in the crossfire. "She should be in the role of best-liked, but she ends up as leader.''[9] And that is in direct contradiction to even the definition of wife: "the hidden or veiled person.''[10] So the many wives who are now in the work force, exposed to the world at large like their husbands, are contradicting their own positions in marriage. They are not settled solely into their domestic role, and even if they are otherwise traditional and do not seek authority, their chances of being happy in marriage are slim because they have broken with that conservative group that succeeds best in marriage. Thus they are more likely to be' among that majority who show up in divorce court after the first year, or to be the one in four who is divorced by the 7th year.[11] And if the housewife is bored with her domestic duties and role as "best-liked" person, she may be among the annual 3,600 run-away wives in Canada.[12]

If numbers constitute normality, the dissolved marriage is normal; that is not a very good average for humanity's "basic adult relationship." And a look at some typical "happy" marriages reveals that marriage must be a system that is no longer valid; it is not meeting the needs of the individuals involved. As H. L. Mencken puts it, "Who are happy in marriage? Those with so little imagination that they cannot picture a better state, and those so shrewd that they prefer quiet slavery to hopeless rebellion.''[13] But if the people involved in these so-called happy mar-

62

riages are in reality shallow, dull, bored, trapped, and presenting a front to the world, why do two million couples continue to enter into this contract every year?[14] Why do they voluntarily enter into a life of wage-slavery, status slavery and sex-slavery, especially when the domestic role of the female is unlikely to be fulfilling?

For the woman, especially, this is explained by the fact that "real life is what she sees in the pictures, not what's happening around her."[15] She is blind to her mother's loneliness and isolation. She does not see that marriage means she will abandon her loyalty to other females, that she will subordinate all other relationships to the one with her husband, but that he will have it both ways. " . . . he has a marriage affiliation and a male affiliation . . . . A man talking to another man thinks of himself as an individual; a woman talking to another woman is more likely to think of herself as a member of a marriage."[16]

What force is it that closes young men and women's eyes to the unhappiness of their parents or makes them believe they can avoid the pitfalls of their parents' generation? Jessie Bernard, points out that the "professed reason for getting married is likely to be that 'we are in love.' This is part of the romantic myth of our culture. Love is the conventional reason for getting married; it is simulated if not felt; it is the 'correct thing.' "[17] Love, not a desire to enter into a legal, economic contract or a quest for companionship or any of the other positive motivations toward marriage is the conscious reason most people marry. Its influence on the young's concept of marriage has led to widespread early marriage. In 1969, the latest year for which figures are available, 806 girls *under* 15 were married.[18] The typical bride is only 20.5 years old, and has finished only 2.8 years of high school.[19] These young women are willing to eliminate any hope of being financially self-supporting and to thus increase their chances of being among the 50% of all divorce cases that involve those who marry before their twentieth year because, in the name of romantic love, everything is permissible. Never mind the statistics; "its bigger than both of us."[20] In our case, things will work out because we have found true love.

Here is what a noted social philosopher, Ralph Linton, says about these romantic ideas. "All societies recognize that there are occasional violent emotional attachments between persons of opposite sex, but our present American culture is practically the only one which has attempted to capitalize these and make them the basis for marriage, most groups regard them as unfortunate and point out the victims of such attachments as horrible examples. Their rarity in most societies suggests that they are psychological abnormalities to whom our own culture has attached an extraordinary value just as other cultures have attached extreme values to other abnormalities."[21] Are we to believe that what sociologist call the basic human institution originated in an abnormality? If so, why does marriage exist in these other societies?

The entire concept of love has played a dual, and contradictory, role in marriage. On the one hand, it has become the professed reason for marriage, and it has become so dominant that it is vital to experience love to be considered normal. Happiness and fulfilment are non-existent, especially for the female, unless she has loved and married. And of course, most are so anxious to be normal that they are forced to capitalize on their sexual attractiveness to the utmost, so that they will be ranked as 'popular' by their peers. The earlier they marry, the sooner they prove they are normal. On the other hand, love has raised the expectations lovers have of marriage so much that it has contributed to the low chances for success in that institution. Love has grossly oversold marriage.

"Expecting more than was reasonable, young people have been doomed to disillusionment from the start. Their inflated hopes, incapable of fulfilment, were found to be shattered .... the romantic conception of marriage has pictured it as the panacea for all life's ills, an idyllic state into which harassed men and women might withdraw from life's struggles to find solace and healing .... Marriage is a good, and a rewarding relationship. But it cannot deliver goods matched to this kind of anticipation."[22] So the quest for love rushes people into marriage while simultaneously raising their hopes so high that they can only become disillusioned. A few may make a realistic adjustment and work out an arrangement, but the *young* newlyweds are not prepared to make such adjustments; they just think they chose a partner poorly.

The sociologists explain away this pattern of early marriages as being caused by "puppy love, infatuation, romantic love, platonic love ... such love is *immature* love, in that the needs being fulfilled are unreal and are too limited to enhance intellectual and emotional development."[23] True, but the problem with this explanation is that it implies that such a thing as eternal love does exist and so allows young couples to believe they may have found the "real thing." Love is not by definition a mystical, all-powerful, eternal force; the western concept of love in marriage has been invented. According to Webster, love is a feeling of strong personal attachment induced by sympathetic understanding; it is tender and passionate affection for one of the opposite sex. Such feelings do exist, but we should recognize them for what they are. "We have the capacity for dependence which is sometimes mistaken for love. We also have the capability of feeling warmth and affection for a certain person at a certain time, but there's no reason to believe that these feelings won't change as we change. We have very real needs to wield power and to achieve recognition, and those are frequently misnamed love too. We feel pride and gratitude, and sexual attraction, all of which also masquerade under the label of love."[24]

It is ridiculous to enter into a life-time contract, which cannot easily be terminated at will, for a concept as nebulous as love. But millions still do, because the foundations of marriage were laid in the economic structure that is still the basis of western civilization. Men and women are harmed and disappointed by the remnants of the institution of marriage, but they continue to go along with it in the name of love because they do not see it for what it is ... an economic contract, and because, culturally, they believe they can satisfy their sexual desires only in marriage.

Marriage is an economic contract because the husband, in return for household services, is morally obliged to support his wife (and children). But because of the sexist laws that pervade our culture, he is not legally obliged to provide decent support. According to the law, *sex* is the purpose of marriage, as you must engage in sexual intercourse to validate a marriage. But love and affection, those driving forces behind today's marriages, are not required; lack of love is *not* grounds for divorce, but a woman's inability to engage in sexual intercourse is definitely grounds. This is because her status gives her husband privileges that he has contracted to obtain. "A sum of money paid to wife for the weekly budget is the same act as money paid another woman for other purposes, but sociologically they have entirely different meanings. In the one case (the wife's), the payment means a home, loyalty, sexual privilege, responsibility, status, children, obligations to rear these children according to fixed rules and regulations."[25]

The single family is the "economic unit of society"[26] and the reason people enter into marriage thinking it is something besides an economic contract is that is confused with the pair-bond which is still with this species. That pair-bond has now been disguised by the concept of "love" which from the time of the

Greeks until the Victorian era had nothing to do with marriage,[27] thus indicating that the pair-bond and monogamous marriage are indeed something quite different.

Attempts to convince women that they have been indoctrinated to want marriage and that there is no need for it have met little concrete results because of the failure to recognize the existence of this pairing tendency as a biological fact. What must be explained is that there is no need to enter into the obligations and responsibilities of a marriage and to accept the subservient position as a woman therein. What must be shown is that "the bargain in today's unwritten marriage contract is that the husband gets the right to the wife's services in return for supporting her . . . and that he has the *absolute* right to the product of the wife's industry within the home,"[28] even if she is otherwise employed. What must be acknowledged is that there is a great urge to form that partnership in the first place. From there on progress toward the realization of the unfairness and obsolescence of the existing marriage contract will be swifter. The terms of this contract are obsolete because they are the basis of an economic system that has always meant the exploitation of all except the few, including the subjugation of women and children.

The trend, still quite small and facing many legal barriers, of a couple writing their own contract is a reasonable next step. It must be kept in mind, however, that the biological tendency to pair was formed when life-spans were extremely short; therefore the pair bonds that are formed should not be expected to last a present life-time. Besides, there are new factors involved, such as overpopulation and extensive leisure time. The pair-bond originally evolved to save a threatened species; unless it now becomes a bond based on psychological needs rather than merely sexual ones — barring effective and accepted birth control — the species will evolve beyond the pair-bond to ensure survival. What about the question of shortened work weeks and extensive leisure time? Can any couple expect to benefit from one another's companionship for such extended periods over 50 or 60 years? I think not. Perhaps what will occur is a series of pair-bonds, much like the series of marriages and divorces of today. Or, such a partnership could last if the members fully recognize and respect the other's right to know other people of the same or opposite sex — in any way.

Children have been used to keep women tied to domestic tasks and also to limit her contact with other men (and women) because of the overriding drive of the man to ensure that he was the father of the children who would inherit from him. And the woman was almost *required* to have children — for a while, wives in Greece, for example, were only needed to produce legitimate children, even if they were not suited for such work. A release from the bondage of marriage would then allow only those women and men who want to have children to have them, although for many other reasons not relevant here, the desire to have children should not constitute the right to raise them. Because offspring has been man's ticket to eternity, children have been commodities to display. This contributed to virtually every psychosis, neurosis, and character disorder imaginable. So that final argument that "children need marriage"[29] is no argument at all.

In fact, no one does.

Notes

1. Herman R. Lantz and Eloise C. Snyder, *Marriage: An examination of the Man-Woman Relationship*, John Wiley & Sons, Toronto, 1969, p. 16.
2. *Ibid.,* p. 106.
3. *Ibid.,* pp. 82-83.
4. *Ibid.,* p. 222.
5. *Ibid.,* p. 59.
6. David and Vera Mace, *Marriage: East and West,* Doubleday and Company, New York, 1960, p. 328.
7. *Ibid.,* p. 322.
8. *Ibid.,* p. 330.
9. *Ibid.*
10. Ruth Dickson, *Marriage is a Bad Habit,* Sherbourne Press, Los Angeles, 1968, p. 11.
11. Cf. *ibid.,* p. 20.
12. Cf. Carl Dow, "Why Thousands of Wives are Running Away," *Weekend Magazine,* Canada, November 20, 1971.
13. Quoted from Dickson, *op. cit.,* p. 33.
14. Cf. *ibid.,* p. 21.
15. *Ibid.,* p. 30.
16. Philip E. Slater, "Must Marriage Cheat Today's Young Women," *Redbook,* February 1971, p. 166.

17. Mace, *op. cit.*, p. 314.
18. Cf. Dickson, *op. cit.*, pp. 19 & 27.
20. *Ibid.*, p. 74.
21. Mace, *op. cit.*, p. 313.
22. *Ibid.*, pp. 324-325.
23. Lantz, *op. cit.*, p. 107.
24. Dickson, *op. cit.*, pp. 84-85.
25. Carl C. Zimmermann, *Family and Civilization*, Harper, New York, p. 14.
26. Friedrich Engels, *The Origin of The Family, Private Property and the State*, International Publishers, New York, 1942, p. 149.
27. Dickson, *op. cit.*, pp. 87-98.
28. Susan Edmiston, "How to Write Your Own Marriage Contract," *MS*, Spring, 1972, p. 68.
29. Dickson, *op. cit.*, p. 57.

YOU KNOW THE TYPE

Turn down the lamp love
and let's go to bed
but first walk the dog love
You heard what I said.
Turn down the lamp love
when you've locked the door
and put out the cat love
that's just one thing more.
Do you want some tea love
with cinnamon bread?
You do love?
Then bring some
up here to bed!
Don't leave the lamp love
remember the bill
and now that you're here love
will you take the pill

Mary Yuill

MEDIA (and women)

they, afraid mankind be hermaphroditic
    like a worm,
will demand of woman to expose through her dress
    her maidenhood
to prove to the sexless 20th century
        their senile fertility.

mary melfi, 1971

WOMEN IN ADVERTISING

by

Katherine McGillivray

I'm fed up to my head and shoulders with advertising that insults women. And I'm also puzzled, to the tips of my Revlon-painted toenails, by an advertising approach that holds 51% of its customers in utter contempt. We are shown as kitchen lackeys — and while the woman does the menial work, there's a man doing the voice over. Man sells, woman slaves.

The time has come for advertising men to liberate themselves from their false idea of women. Don't they realize how many working-age women are out working today? Half the women in the country are simply not at home when The Fag with A Bag — I mean, the Man from Glad — drops in. They're at their desks, their factory benches, or their seats in the Boardroom.

Now, I really don't think that all advertisers are male chauvinist pigs, but I do think that they're missing out on their market. Contempt for their female 51% of the buying public leads them into some very curious advertising. Do they really think we believe in fairies? Like that awful Man from Glad? Do they think we sit at home, hoping Mr. Clean and those other weirdos will drop by?

When they go home to their wives and girlfriends, do they ask them: "Seen the White Knight today, honey?" Do they look out of their picture windows and shout: "Hey! It's a white tornado!" If not, why not? If they don't talk to their own women that way, why do they do so to the rest of us?

Why have they created this extraordinary image of us? How long will it be before they liberate us women from this hopelessly distorted picture they present of us? It had better be soon. For

I believe that this liberation is a great deal more important than they seem to imagine.

What kind of homes are advertisers forcing upon us? With floors that mustn't be stepped on, kitchens where nobody cooks, with an atmosphere like a hospital ward.

Correction. Somebody is allowed to cook — but only grandma. And only cake-mix. You see the old bag leering over her steel-rimmed glasses. Mother doesn't cook. She serves. She serves Instant Breakfast to a bunch of layabouts who can't crawl out of bed ten minutes earlier to get to the office or school on time. She beams with motherly pride as her children stuff their faces with food. She's forever shoving food down people. Usually cheap food, closely followed by expensive aspirins and remedies for acid indigestion. Which is probably why one seldom sees her eating.

Even when there's a party, she's there with her tray. Fetching and carrying like crazy. Then her husband turns round and shouts at her because she's bought bitter coffee. Or the Ajax has turned blue. Or she's starched his socks. And her daughter whines: "Wouldn't you know — my big chance! A date with George, and I'm all out of mouthwash!" What a crew. My grandmother the cake-mix cook. My husband Attila the Hun. My son the gobbler. My daughter the Gargler. Family life of a wife and mother, courtesy of the advertising industry.

Thanks a whole lot. We haven't come as far as you might think, baby. We've still a helluva way to go.

Have they ever stopped to think of the overall picture this approach presents of Canadian womanhood? A sort of white female Stepin Fetchit, a lackey chained to her kitchen, with under-arms like the Sahara, her scalp as flake-less as a billiard ball, breathing hexachlorophine over the Man from Glad, comparing the whiteness of washes from dawn till dusk with some seedy idiot with a microphone, doling out cardboard cornflakes and great dollops of monosodium glutamate and carrying plates, carrying trays, carrying, carrying. Not much of a picture, is it? No wonder so many daughters, alarmed at the prospect of living like this, are taking off to communes.

So far, I've done nothing but complain about the image advertising men have created of women. But now I'm going to unburden myself of some advice which, if followed — and I have no reason to doubt that it will — will liberate us women from where we sit. At the bottom of our broken pedestals. Here's what advertisers can do for us. Show us as intelligent human beings, not as if

72

we had all had prefrontal lobotomies.

Stop portraying us as ill-mannered witches who sneer at the whiteness (or non-whiteness) of each other's laundry and sniff for cabbage smells. Show us with a reasonable standard of human behavior and decent feelings.

Stop talking down to women. Talk *to* us.

REMEMBERING GERMAINE GREER'S VISIT
by
Mary Riopel

Prior to the birth of the current Women's Liberation Movement, "chauvinism" was rarely seen in popular magazines, paperbacks or daily newspapers; now, it must be admitted, the word is fast becoming trite from over-use. My 85-year-old Thesaurus lists about forty other words and phrases that can be used in its stead and, it seems to me, "cock-a-hoopness" is the one most descriptive of the flight into absurdity of some Canadian newsmen during Germaine Greer's visit here in October, 1971.

The first indication that this male affliction was abroad in the land came with an article in the *Montreal Star,* where, in bold, black, half-inch letters, a veteran journalist wrote:

SIX-FOOT GERMAINE CASHES IN ON WOMEN'S LIB

One can't help wondering whether the man thinks there ought to be a specific height above which women should not be permitted to grow, or that people who "cash in" on radical issues (such as newspapermen) are, by Jove, an overly materialistic, almost repugnant, lot.

The lead, "Germaine Greer has achieved the ultimate in liberation — a woman who is paid to talk," was acceptable, if clichéd humour. But I'm sure most people would agree that his rude, derogatory remarks about her physical appearance were not: "Her hair suffers from terminal frizzies; she wears her chest at half-mast and about a trowel and a half of pancake makeup; she walks like Alec Guinness, plucks her eyebrows, and has a Nat King Cole-sized mouth.''

Then, after wallowing in a verbal quagmire himself, the worldly writer turns puritan and takes umbrage at the lady's use of that less-than-genteel, four-letter word — a verb that is not only quite acceptable in male circles but also tends to bestow an aura of savoir-faire on the user.

The balance of the article was not particularly original, but interspersed with a good deal of fuming trivia were undocumentable declarations like, ''the last thing most men want is subservient clinging wives,'' and ''the silent majority of housewives are happily married.'' (The latter assertion obviously indicates shocking male cock-a-hoopness, since Freud himself, after countless years of study of the female libido, could provide no prognosis of what it takes to make a woman happy.)

The next media personality to succumb to the epidemic was a usually well-mannered, jack-of-all-programs, and star performer on a lively, informative CTV daily show. But during the interview with Dr. Greer on October 31st, this gentleman changed character completely and, with the smirk of an acned adolescent hiding a copy of *Playboy,* asked a puzzled Germaine, ''Is it true you never wear a bra?'' And, ''Are you wearing one today?''

(Note: What makes this a classic case of rank cock-a-hoopness is that he did not ask the male guests if they wore jock straps!)

But who could have anticipated that Women's Lib protagonists would be provided with ammunition at the National level? On the contrary, it was natural to assume that CBC would at last provide a decorous forum where Dr. Greer's acknowledged gift for intelligent debate and humorous repartee would enjoy free rein. This was a valid expectation since the moderator was to be a veteran interviewer who has refereed some very radical (male) TV confrontations with admirable skill and objectivity.

Ostensibly, Germaine was to cross swords with an ex-Manitoba M.P. But, once the formal introductions had been made, the moderator acted like a Daughter Of The American Revolution suddenly confronted with Rap Brown in the raw, and threw professional unbias to the winds. His sudden verbal assault on Dr. Greer was not only irrational, but (worse) she was given no chance to even consider, much less debate, his passionately-held anti-Womens Lib convictions.

It must be admitted, however, that the program was not a complete loss, as the former M.P., looking for all the world like a startled doe from whom a succulent morsel of bark has been rudely snatched, was, for once in his vociferous political career, utterly dumbfounded.

It is most unlikely the highly intelligent, impish Germaine Greer was unduly surprised by all this weird, immature, male behaviour. But once again Canadian women were exposed to a shameless exhibition of male cock-a-hoopness in its most blatant, elemental form.

THE QUESTION OF EMPLOYMENT

There are many women who are already bitten by the poisonous fly of parasitism.

Nellie McClung, 1916

In 1970, 85.4% of all single women aged 15 to 34 were in the labour force; 32 % of all married women were in the labour force.

Women's Bureau,
Canada Department of Labour, 1971

IT IS THE EMPLOYER'S FAULT

by

Edith Murphy

On December 9th, 1970, an article appeared in the Montreal *Gazette* entitled "It's Not The Employers Fault." The article refers to comments made by the Royal Commission on The Status Of Women In Canada, which criticize the practices of chartered banks and department stores as major sources of employment for women. The article is full of distortions and half-truths which I would like to investigate here.

My comments refer only to department stores, since I can talk about these from first hand experience. This industry lends itself by tradition and inclination to a high preponderance of women employees and though, at the lower levels, we find women performing many tasks as sales people, clerks, sectionheads and minor supervisors, the management and policy-setting body is overwhelmingly male. Management is to blame for this to a very great extent, because women who would be capable are not given the training or experience to broaden their knowledge and insights. However, it must be said that women have in the past hindered their own advancement by not taking an interest in acquiring skills, by not wanting responsibilities which go with decision making and by accepting their given status meekly and without opposition.

Women do not receive equal wages for equal work. For the past two years, a half-hearted attempt has been made to equalize salaries. This small gain can be attributed to women's new awareness of themselves and to the power they are learning to exert. But equal pay for equal work is still a matter of the employer's good will and not primarily a matter of right. Many categories are invented and differences thought up to prevent equality.

In our society, a person's worth often depends on his financial status. This way of looking upon people is particularly prevalent in the business community. Salary therefore is used to manipulate workers and particularly women workers. Women are a cheap source of labor. Industry is not going to give up this advantage readily. Legislation is badly needed. Vigilance on the part of women is equally important, for industry helps to perpetuate the myth that women are naturally inferior: by paying women less, by presuming that certain positions do not suit woman's abilities.

Though management gives lip-service to equal pay, it channels women into positions where in fact they do not have the opportunity to better their financial position. For instance, few women are working in the lucrative straight commission departments. Women are actually discouraged from competing for these positions. They are placed in departments where the work is of a routine nature. They are not advised that it is desirable and necessary for career-growth to be moved occasionally. Female salesclerks usually remain where they have been originally placed. 25 years of experience in selling scarves and gloves — who needs it?

It is now common practice to hire both men and women at the same wage, but it is still not general to place women in areas where they will be taught skills of salesmanship enabling them to get a better than average paycheck.

A certain store's personnel spokesman admits to hiring more men then women for management training positions. "But the choice between a man and a woman depends on the position to be filled," he says, "eventually we will have young women supervisors in fashions, but not in departments like hardware." He concludes by saying that, at higher levels, it makes no difference and that there are women at that level. This statement is very contradictory, and also happens to be untrue. How do women get to the top if they are limited to fashions only, at lower levels of management? Women must first be trained in the many facets of merchandising, accounting, controlling, and operation of a plant if they are to advance to higher levels. This training is not available if women can only hold fashion positions. Therefore the higher levels of which this spokesman speaks are still in the area of junior, or at best middle management level.

The actual practice, in most Montreal department stores, is to hire management trainees at unequal salaries for male and female, with a 30% higher salary for males. The women are then placed in fashion oriented departments and the men are placed in all positions, including fashions. Because of this greater mobility and their correspondingly greater economic value to the firm, they quickly surpass women in wages, which were never equal to begin with, and also attain positions of command.

In one Montreal department store, policies have changed within the past two years. Previously women were always hired at 20 to 30% less salary than men, regardless of the job which had to be filled and of whether they were line for management positions. Today, at least the basic wages are the same for both sexes. However the equalization stops there. Here also women are not given equality of training, beyond the basic premerchandising course which all new management trainees must successfully complete as a condition of their employment. Here also most female recruits are steered toward the fashion oriented departments. I was told by a personnel spokesman that this is the women's own choice, and not the company's!

Another frequently evoked problem in employing female staff is that of turnover. Another myth. My own observations are that men and women either stay or leave for the same reasons. If they are satisfied with their employment conditions and their wages they are apt to stay. If their job satisfies their psychological needs and helps to fulfil them as people they are apt to stay. This is true of both sexes. Why then have women gained the reputation of instability in the job market?

Primarily because industry has not helped them solve their problems of child-bearing and child-rearing. And because industry does not want to recognise that, today, women are contributing to industry in a meaningful, creative way; and because industry only admits to a menial contribution from its women workers. Woman is allowed to perform routine and boring tasks, because she is easily replaceable in these. Women, it should be noted, manage to fulfill their work responsibilities to a remarkable extent, as the Royal Commission reported:

> Women are absent about two days more than men in a year. This difference seems too slight to have any bearing on the future success or failure of an employee. We wonder whether an employer would choose between two men employees on this basis.[1]

As for turnover, here is a report from a Montreal department store, quoted by the Royal Commission:

> Findings of studies in turnover rates of women and men are far from conclusive. The effect of sex is hard to isolate from other factors such as age, education, marital status, industry and place of employment. Level of employment is sometimes relevant because employees

at routine levels and in dead-end jobs have less stake in a career .... Most studies indicate that women are absent from work more often than men, but this may be related to their job level rather than their sex. Some studies indicate that employees in the lower income brackets have higher absentee rates than those in the upper brackets. The question is whether absentee rates in the low income brackets are higher because women are predominantly there, or whether women's absentee rates are higher because they are routine low-level jobs.[2]

This study has proven that turnover is not high simply because of women employees. On the contrary, there is a very good possibility that firms initiate the turnover, because they do not allow their female workers to escape from low-level jobs.

Some progress appears to have been made during the last two years. This is due not so much to the generosity of the establishment, as it is due to the fact that retailing is extremely sensitive to public opinion. Public opinion is becoming increasingly more sympathetic to women's self-determination. However, once employed, women are still guided into dead end jobs. This is true at all levels. A sales "lady" is not taught the added skill necessary to place her in a department where her own efforts dictate the size of her pay check.

Management only communicates those items it considers proper and there is a great deal of secrecy about the amount of salary a job is worth, or the status to which one is entitled. Management will have to give some thought to training capable women, through job rotation and on the job training. It is not true that women have less mobility. I know dozens of women who are mobile, who are divorced, separated, who have not been married or who are married, and who are capable and loyal employees. I therefore say that woman's lack of mobility is a fixation perpetuated by management.

As for as absenteeism and turnover, I have found this to be a matter of morale, rather than sex. Women who are content with their jobs and find pleasure in what they are doing, will not leave or be absent any more than men. It has been my experience, as an executive who has worked with both sexes, that women have a very strong sense of responsibility, and that given the chance to exercise it, they do so with excellent results. Equality of opportunity is a myth perpetuated by personnel management, which by the way, in most cases, does not contain a single woman at the decision-making level. Only four short years ago female university graduates were completely excluded from on-campus interviews by a Montreal firm.

Are we to believe that all prejudice has been wiped out in the interim, and that today there exists complete equality of opportunity? The evidence is overwhelmingly against such supposition and proves *it is the employer's fault* that women are not given the chance for better jobs. (Further evidence can be found in the Royal Commission Report, as well as in its sub-report, *Patterns of Manpower Utilization in Canadian Department Stores,* prepared by Marianne Bossen.)

Notes

1. *Report of The Royal Commission on The Status of Women in Canada,* Information Canada, Ottawa, 1970, p. 95.
2. *Ibid.,* pp. 94-95.

WOMEN
AND THE ARTS:
Criticism
and
Poetry

FEMINIST CRITICISM

by

Margret Andersen

A few colleagues and I were discussing one day the choice of a guest speaker for a yearly lecture which is supposed to examine literary problems of interest to the entire university community. Several names were proposed, all of them male. I mentioned Mary Ellmann — "Who is that?", asked one of my learned (male) colleagues, while another (male) inquired whether she was Richard Ellmann's wife. When I informed them of the existence of Mary Ellmann's book, *Thinking About Women,*[1] a certain perplexedness seemed to seize the group, soon to be succeeded, however, by general amusement when one of the gentlemen decided it would be easier not to think about women right there and then.

I wonder how many people, learned or not, but interested in literature, have read *Thinking About Women*. A "luminous book," says Ashley Montagu, "usefully embarrassing to the male reader," admits P. J. Kavanagh, "a funny feminist book," concludes Sidney Callahan. I suppose it takes (a woman) more than that to convince my (male) colleagues. I wonder how many people have read another quite outstanding exercise in feminist criticism, namely *The School of Femininity,* by Margaret Lawrence[2], who analyses in this study approximately sixty-five women novelists and the female writer in general. These are two excellent books, yet many of us, even of us women, do not know about them, have not read them.

Why is this so? Why has literary criticism, for so many years, been an almost exclusively male field? Why do works and achievements by women occupy so small a place in the curricula of our schools? It is my opinion that many are reluctant, or even afraid, to investigate the question of the creative potential of women, reluctant to discover the reality of past and present injustices, afraid to encounter a hidden strength which might well destroy accepted patterns of thought.

It is never easy to introduce fundamental changes into one's *Weltanschauung*. Events in political or private life may lead or force one to accept such changes, but there is a scarcity of people who will accept them voluntarily or who will actively search for possibilities of change. Consequently, it is not easy to become a feminist. It is even frightening, for the understanding of the feminist cause means changes in all domains of life, political and private.

Indeed it is sometimes quite painful to be a feminist. When you cannot see *Hamlet* anymore without giving much of your attention to Ophelia and to the cavalier way in which she is treated by both her father and her lover; when you become annoyed with yourself for still humming the German folksong (written by Goethe) "Sah ein Knab' ein Röslein steh'n" which tells the story of a beautiful but helpless maiden who cannot defend herself against the male aggressor; when Camus suddenly is no longer flawless in your eyes because of his failure to see woman other than in her relationship to man, then, indeed, something quite grave has happened.

It becomes evident that your new way of thinking has invaded you totally. So far, you had probably objected to certain attitudes of relatives, colleagues, friends, foes, you had seen discrimination and sexism in education, law, customs, public life, advertising etc. But now, you are beginning to discover it also in works of art that you used to cherish. The critic in you can no longer avoid taking into account a new dimension — your feminine consciousness — and the 'musée imaginaire,' which used to be your ultimate refuge, is not safe anymore, is in need of renovation, as everything it houses becomes subject to your feminist critique.

In a way, of course, this painful process leads also to a rejuvenation of the mind, of your eyes, ears, of your feelings. You do discover new friends, in your everyday reality as well as in what goes beyond it. This then is the constructive side of feminist criticism.

Let me give you an example: I had always been somewhat reluctant to read with any serious interest the works of Colette. (Both for my M.A. and my Ph.D. theses, I attacked such literary (male) giants as Proust and Claudel.) Somehow, in my snobism, I did not like the titles of Colette's novels — *Gigi, Claudine . . ., Chéri,* etc. I had thought of their author as a facile and therefore popular woman novelist. Recently, Colette became one of the writers I have newly discovered for myself. Henri Peyre speaks in his excellent study, *French Novelists of Today* of the "striking flowering of French feminine fiction."[3] I am wondering whether the use of the word 'flowering' is not again an example of 'phallic criticism.' Women are flowers to so many men, the metaphor of the rose has been used over and over again (Goethe, Thackeray, Saint-Exupéry, just to name three offenders). Sematology must also become one of the tools of feminism; I question the word flowering in this context. Peyre adds that "easily half of the talents in French fiction and short story, since 1930 or so, have been women."[4] However, only one of the twelve chapters of Peyre's book deals with the writings of women, altogether 30-40 pages. Fourteen of these pages furthermore deal with Simone de Beauvoir only, which does not leave much space for other authors. We must conclude that Peyre needs only 15 pages to deal with "half of the talents" since 1930, the female half, and that the male half of the talents is dealt with much more fairly. I used to admire Henri Peyre for his work, I still do, but it is an admiration mixed with disillusion and regret.

Undoubtedly, some will reject the idea of consciousness-raising in the field of literary criticism and will belittle the idea, as the feminist cause is belittled in so many fields. Of course, impartial and impassionate criticism is what we all have stood for, in the past. But let us not forget that much of the impartial criticism has often be passionately biased. We have accepted critics of pronounced religious (Pierre-Henri Simon) or political (George Lucàcs) convictions. Why not accept a feminist outlook which will contribute to the elucidation of other aspects of literary works?

I certainly do not want to read women writers only, nor do I want to limit my enjoyment of the visual arts to the works of women artists only. Nevertheless, a compensatory program of study and reflection seems in order. A woman discovers herself more easily in the company and with the help of other women. It is not only helpful but also necessary for me to become acquainted with what I have ignored for so long. I must become more familiar with the female artist and the female thinker, before I can try to build for myself a new imaginary museum in which both men and women will hold their place. What I am proposing is an enrichment and not a impoverishment of knowledge.

Phallic criticism, as Mary Ellmann so wittily calls it, has existed for a long time. It will have to learn to co-exist with vulvate criticism. In *les Guérillères*[5], a sort of epic singing the future glory of woman, Monique Wittig sees the vulva as a beautiful object, as an object of cult, a cult based on the teachings of a bible called *Féminaire*. Like this French novelist, women critics now tend to counter 'phallic criticism' with a criticism marked by woman's pride in her sex. In her foreword to *The School of Feminity,* Margaret Lawrence defines her book as following a definite pattern of thought, namely "that women for the first time in history upon a large scale are saying their particular say about themselves, about men, and about life as it treats them separately and together with men."[6] It is high time for literary criticism to take this phenomenon into account.

I do not propose that there be two distinct branches of criticism, one by, for and on men, the other by, for and on women. But we, both men and women, must stop treating books by women "as though they themselves were women"[7], as though "there must always be two literatures like two public toilets, one for men and one for women."[8] 'Phallic criticism' has served and is still serving to perpetuate the myth of the artistic (and other) inferiority of women; consequently, 'vulvate criticism' seems, at the present time, justified as a weapon to combat this myth.

As long as the words feminine and woman writer are used as pejorative qualifications, such combat is necessary, just as necessary as 'la querelle des anciens et des modernes' in seventeenth century French thought. Feminism and feminist critique will not simply 'go away', the 'fad', as many hopefully call feminism, will not fade out. 'Les anciens et les modernes' will have to arrive at an understanding, in order to allow the streams of male and female consciousness to converge into the river of human consciousness.

Notes

1. Harcourt, Brace, Jovanovich, New York, 1968.
2. Frederick A. Stokes, New York, 1936.
3. Oxford University Press, New York, 1967.
4. *Ibid.,* p. 292.
5. Editions de Minuit, Paris, 1969.
6. p. xii.
7. Mary Ellmann, *op. cit.,* p. 29.
8. *Ibid.,* p. 33.

LETTERS TO . . .

by

Margret Andersen

Women are often said to be letter-writers *par excellence*. In his *Histoire de la Littérature Féminine en France*[1], Jean Larnac explains how women progressed from the art of writing letters — Madame de Sévigné — to that of writing novels — George Sand. He assures us that poetry, especially non-lyrical, hermetic poetry, as well as the drama must because of their more abstract character, remain genres with which women cannot deal.

His theory is arrogant, and chauvinistic; it is a theory which discriminates both against women and certain literary forms. According to it, women have written letters (or epistolic novels) because, with their inferior minds, they could handle this inferior form. Women, according to Larnac's findings, were able to invade the field of the novel because, except when written by men, the novel is an easier literary genre.

Of course, some great men, Voltaire for instance, have also enjoyed being epistolists. Indeed, most critics will agree that Voltaire's *Correspondance* is far more more interesting than his theatre or his efforts in the epic genre. But notice the difference: the letters of great men become great correspondences; the letters of women remain letters, however 'charming' and 'moving.' *Les Lettres de Madame de Sévigné* reveal, says Larnac, her "'génie du bavardage.'"[2] A striking example of 'phallic criticism.'

I do not know what the last bastion of literary male chauvinism will be. We must presume that it will be the drama, for women have, in the meantime, written quite remarkable poetry and fiction.

Let me offer a different explanation for the apparent preference given by woman writers to the genres of letter and novel. It could well be that women feel, in a particularly haunting manner, the need to communicate with others. That from woman's isolated place in the home, letter and novel were better means of communication with friends and with the large number of women who, during the nineteenth century and in the isolation of their own homes, became avid readers of novels.

A poem, this condensed expression of emotion and thought, is perhaps destined to be communication with the 'happy few' only. And the theatre, of course, remains even today more a privilege of the well-to-do. Furthermore, a woman will read a novel by herself; most women attend plays in the company of men.

Let us then not consider the letter and the novel an easy solution of an author's problems, but rather a more effective way of reaching out to others.

At a time when letters are being replaced by telephone conversations, when the "génie du bavardage" of Madame de Sévigné could never have developed in written form, some women decided to address themselves directly to artists of the past whose works were offensive to their feminine consciousness. Following are excerpts from this aesthetic correspondence, as well as a number of critiques in the usual form.

Notes

1. Editions Krâ, Paris, 1929.
2. *Op. cit.*, p. 111.

LETTER TO ANTOINE DE SAINT-EXUPÉRY:

For over twenty-five years your *Little Prince* was one of my favorite books. I found it to be a book of friendship, love, care and sentiment. I found it to be frankly emotional, containing no intellectual pretentions. Having been asked to analyse a children's book for a course in Women's Studies, it was natural to turn to you, Saint-Exupéry. I hoped to be able to point out that one can talk about love without talking about male or female, or maybe I would just reread the book to get into the mood, ending up by borrowing books from my granddaughter to write this exercise. And so I started to read, charmed and enchanted as always by the prose, the pictures and the sentiment, until I came to page 31, when, all of a sudden, I underwent a profound shock. Never before did I realize that you do indeed talk about male and female; never before did I perceive the patronizing, no, I must call it the insulting attitude you adopted vis-à-vis women. What else have I been reading, studying and accepting without question? How many insults and slanders have I not recognized, have I not been aware of?

Flowers on the little prince's planet were very simple, inoffensive and quick to fade, until the rose was born. She is not satisfied to be timid and modest, but emerges with much coquettishness and vanity, petal by petal, from her green chamber. "It was only in the full radiance of her beauty that she wished to appear."[1] The little prince has a great deal of trouble with his rose, because she is spoiled and has many whims. She is vain and so the little prince comes to look on her as being a very complex creature. The rose embellishes herself and her existence with such obvious untruth, that the little prince, though he professes to love her, soon comes to doubt her. This makes him very sad, because he had taken seriously words which were without importance. "One never ought to listen to flowers. One should simply look at them and breath their fragrance ... I did not know how to take pleasure in all her grace. This tale of claws which disturbed me so much, should only have filled my heart with tenderness and pity ... I ought to have guessed all the affection that lay behind her poor little strategems. Flowers are so inconsistent ..."[2]

It is now obvious to me that the flowers you wrote about are the females. They are of little consequence, except when they are, like the rose, very beautiful creatures. The ordinary flowers come fast and fade fast. The rose, beautiful in a very calculated way, wants to impress, to be noticed and goes about it in a systematic manner. Vain, very vain, but that is after all a charming way to be, provided it is used to enhance the ego of the lover. Like most women she is empty-headed and talks a lot of nonsense. The little prince discovers that with females one takes pleasure only in the sensual. After all, they are full of inconsistencies, which might fill one with compassion for their incompetence, but should not make one unhappy. Flowers (women) are naive, they need protection, they cannot be responsible for themselves; they are not people in the same way males are people; they are incapable of controlling their own destinies; they must be manipulated for their own good. They are the pleasing, the beautiful, the enrichment of men's life, provided one takes pleasure in their being only and does not try to understand their thought-processes, which in any case cannot be done. These beauties are of course the lesser, the other. The little prince is responsible for his rose. She is weak, naive; she has four useless thorns which she thinks will protect her from the world, but he knows they won't.

Here once more we have the traditional view of woman. Dangerously so, because in this instance it lacks maliciousness and is not blatantly hostile. It is a put-down just the same; like so many others, repeated over and over again. It is not surprising that the principle sinks into everyone's consciousness, male as well as female. Woman must be beautiful and charming, that is her role in life. She does not need to develop her mind, she won't need to use it, she would not know how to use it. She will never have to, will never be able to shoulder responsibility. She will never be a person in her own right, she will be adopted, looked after, patronized and, if she is very beautiful, she will delight the male. We find this concept everywhere, even in our favorite books.

I am sad to have lost faith in so 'charming' a book, but I am pleased also to be able to recognize discrimination wherever I find it. It hurts but it fortifies. And the thorns of the rose gain in value. Those thorns, one of these days, will no longer be useless. I am angry to be your friend no more, Antoine de Saint-Exupéry, but then, I believe, you never were mine.

Edith Murphy

Notes

1. Antoine de Saint-Exupéry, *The Little Prince,* Harbrace Paperbound Library, Harcourt, Brace & World Inc., New York, 1943, p. 33.
2. *Ibid.,* p. 36.

94

LETTER TO HENRI MATISSE

My knowledge of art is limited. But I am told that you, Henri Matisse, once said, "I have attempted to create a crystalline environment for the spirit." In essence, you created your works mainly for their aesthetic qualities. If that is so, then I must tell you that your *Decorative Figure on an Ornamental Background* does not have any aesthetic value for me.

The decorative figure is a woman. I suppose I take more offence with the title of the work than with the painting itself. You place your subject, the woman, amidst tapestries, plants, fruits and a mirror, the symbol of woman's vanity. I find it disturbing that woman should be depicted in such a way. The subject of the painting, the woman, is really only an object. You could have called this picture *Still Life on an Ornamental Background*. Indeed, the woman appears to be two-dimensional and lifeless.

Looking at the work as a whole, there is little to suggest that the subject is a person with feelings or thoughts. I find this extremely irritating, especially when one remembers that the painting was done in 1927, a time when women were definitely not a sedentary, faceless and passive lot. I find this painting to be contextually outside the reality of its time and subsequently degrading to women.

To conclude, I feel that you aptly entitled this work. The subject (or object) is indeed decorative. But I find it outrageous that an artist who consciously thought in terms of aesthetics could call a woman decorative. This is a term that I cannot accept. The nude, be it woman or man, can be aesthetically beautiful and/or sometimes ugly, but never decorative; to depict a person as such is both alarming and artistically hideous.

You may find me biased. I am. I am sometimes beautiful, hopefully never decorative.

Not yours,
Rhona Selick

95

LEONARD COHEN'S WOMEN

by

Dagmar de Venster

Woman is a bitch, broad, pig, slut, whore, shrew, easy piece, ape, trollop, vampire, witch, who is whammed, knocked up, lain, raped, screwed, fucked. Suffering, sex without love, sodomy and undignified death are her lot. Such is the sexual mistreatment of woman in today's best seller.

Leonard Cohen disposes of Edith in the lowest way possible.[1] In a state of depression, after years of living in the subbasement of an apartment building with her husband, she decides to "teach him a lesson." She squeezes into an elevator shaft and the car descends upon her, crushing her to death in a crouching position. Her husband was to have been returning home at that moment, riding in the elevator that killed her, but, too bad for her, it was only a delivery boy. The lesson was a failure. Edith's entire life was a failure. She was raped in a stone quarry at thirteen, married at sixteen, and apparently did nothing with her life apart from acting as a plaything for her husband and his homosexual friend. Memories of Edith reappear throughout the book with detailed accounts of her abnormal sexual activities, which usually took place in her dingy apartment or in the darkness of the sub-basement.

Half a page is devoted to the lust of a man for a thirteen-year-old body:

> I want thirteen-year-olds in my life. Bible King David had one to warm his dying bed. Why shouldn't we associate with beautiful people? Tight, tight, tight, oh, I want to be trapped in a thirteen-year-old life. I know, I know about war and business. I am aware of shit. Thirteen-year-old electricity is very sweet to suck, and I am (or let me be) tender as a hummingbird. Don't I have some hummingbird in my soul? Isn't there something timeless and unutterably light in

96

my lust hovering over a young wet crack in a blur of blond hair? Oh come, hardy darlings, there is nothing of King Midas in my touch, I freeze nothing into money. I merely graze your hopeless nipples as they grow away from me into business problems. I change nothing as I float and sip under the first bra.[2]

Four men — all drunk — pursue Edith into the pine forest and run her to the ground. They laugh at the thirteen-year-old sauvagesse. "They dragged her into the shadows because each man wanted to be somewhat alone. They undressed her, turned her over, twisted her and, when their erections collapsed, they inserted index fingers, pipe stems, ballpoint pens and twigs until the blood streamed down her legs."[3]

Catherine Tekakwitha, more fortunate than Edith, escapes rape and several arranged marriages. She dies, a virgin, at twenty-four. She is, however, mistreated by the author in other ways.

Queen Victoria — the copper statue on Sherbrooke Street — has a bomb placed in the folds of her lap; Queen Elizabeth's designer is criticized for the style of her uniform top. From the native Indian to members of British royalty, no woman escapes the soiled pen of Leonard Cohen.

Do you have an orifice and a pair of breasts? These are the essential if not sole requirements for a female character in a Leonard Cohen novel. Smooth skin helps, too. Intelligence and personality are of no consequence. In *Beautiful Losers* the ratio of 'Did you come' to 'I love you' is approximately ten to one. And the one 'I love you' is mouthed insincerely, devoid of emotion. Orgasm is pursued via any method: natural (not too frequently), the use of artificial devices, the reading of Nazi horrors, the accounts of Indian tortures wrought upon missionaries, and, of course, heterosexual sodomy.

I must concede that this book has shock value (but then, so does an emetic). I find it obscene and offensive to my female personality. Sex is good only when it is dirty sex ...? Fuck!

Notes

1. Cf. Leonard Cohen, *Beautiful Losers,* The Viking Press, New York, 1966.
2. *Ibid.,* p. 73.
3. *Ibid.,* pp. 76-77.

SCIENCE FICTION AND WOMEN

by

Kathy Gower

Though some authors of science fiction must be commended for at least including female characters in their plots, and thus granting woman a place in the future (unlike a vast number of science fiction worlds that seem populated only by men), the image they are projecting includes far too many of today's misconceptions and generalities about the nature of women.

I find it alarming that science fiction writers continue to conceive of a future where women remain subjugated; may we not even imagine our equality in the future?

Frank Herbert's *Dune,* winner of the Hugo and Nebula Awards for best science fiction novel of the year 1965, was widely acclaimed for the depth of characterization of the 'people,' and the world that he created. But the characterization he gives to his females is disturbing and reveals a certain superficiality in his concepts of womanhood. In addition to his little mentioned "common workers" (wives and natives) who carry the heavy burdens of domestic duties, he has created a "woman-only" cult that jars memories of 'woman as witch.'

The "Bene Gesserit cult" in *Dune* has superior powers that are valuable assets to whatever men of state they are assigned to by the Bene Gesserit Mother Superior. Through generations of selective breeding and then training in special skills of minute observation of people's physiological reactions, men endowed with those powers attain a limited ability to read people's thoughts. Herbert alludes to this ability in terms that bring to mind the concept of women having inexplicable supernatural powers which separate them from men and connect them with the devil. For the men of *Dune* fear and admire the Bene Gesserit women, but they also despise them because they are unnatural.

Besides, the Bene Gesserit only assist men in power rather than exercise it in their own right. Their ultimate aim is to successfully initiate a male into the cult, because he would thus become more powerful; all attempts but one have failed due to some innate difference in the abilities of the sexes. *Dune* tells the exploits of that one male Bene Gesserit.

The mistreatment of women in science fiction is also revealed in Piers Anthony's *Macroscope*. He has created two women with distinctive personalities; once again the women are stereotyped according to the male protagonists' reactions to them. One man, Ivo, finally pinned down the "elusive but essential distinction" between the women after observing them for months: "what Afra had was sex appeal; what Beatryx had was femininity."

Let's examine the latter concept first. Beatryx, in her late 30's, is a very stable person who accepts her shortcomings and her position in life with 'good grace.' She is a noble woman, someone to be admired; Anthony respects her. But what is her position? Housewife, of course. When assigning roles on the spacecraft, she knows her role is cooking and laundry. These tasks, plus cultivating and weeding her garden, she does by hand while the "galactic devices for such tasks stood idle." So the human touch is better even if it means the enslavement of women? This "good wife's" greatest asset is that she can intercept and smooth over a developing argument, and thus is essential to the mission of the crew; unfortunately she is also too slow to understand the point of argument.

Further evidence of what femininity is to the author is obvious in the following passages: " . . . she was cheerful and unassuming, encouraging and sympathetic. Ivo could appreciate the reason Groton, no intellectual slouch himself, had passed over the female engineers he might have had and chosen a woman like this. It was the feeling of familiarity, of home, that he needed most when the revelations of the ages shook his fundamental assumption, and she carried about her a pleasing aura of homebody Earth . . . What about the problem of being fit to live with? By *that* definition, Beatryx was the smartest among them."

So we see woman as a refuge against the bitter outside world. Beatryx comforts and calms the more intelligent crew members, who think her devotion to her husband and her extensive but concealed knowledge of the arts are enough to give meaning to her life. She has absolute faith in her husband, who practices astrology "when he gets bothered," but she "never understood all that. I don't have anything." And indeed she doesn't. When

99

LEWIS AND CLARK COLLEGE LIBRARY
PORTLAND, OREGON 97219

faced with a problem she must solve alone, she cannot think for herself; she must come to a conclusion by consciously thinking, "What would Harold say?" She knows her life is empty, and none of Anthony's attempts to build her up into a noble and dynamic person could succeed, as long as he limited her to 'occupation: housewife.'

In the person of Afra we are treated to an intelligent female scientist — at least job discrimination has been somewhat eliminated in Anthony's future — but he presents her as having sex appeal and an unpredictable emotional temperament that make her difficult to be alone with. "She was too bright, too beautiful, too bitter." And "she was loveliest when expressing emotion." Throughout the novel she is referred to in ways that make it difficult to remember she is a topnotch scientist. She seems scatterbrained next to the more dignified (and 'normal') Beatryx. Once again we have a polarity of "types." She is "finicky" and "fretful, impatient . . . and unappreciative of concerns of others." The working girl seems unpleasant and not at all mature; she is "still a girl." Does this imply a warning that if a woman works her other facets of development will lag behind?

During the course of the novel, Afra does mature and becomes someone possible to live and work with, but that does not overshadow the fact that she is treated superficially both by the author and her male companions. On first meeting Afra, Ivo is "embarrassed for Brad's superficiality" in choosing a "starlet type." Ivo takes her at face value just because she is beautiful; if she were not, he probably would have ignored the fact that this scientist was a woman. So apparently Anthony presumes that women will continue to be judged first by their appearance. The first indication of her personality is her room, where the furnishings are "distinctly feminine. Frilly curtains . . . walls wee pastel pink. Brushes and creams lined the surface of the standard desk . . . you knew there was a Lady present."

And listen to this statement made by Harold speaking of Beatryx: "Every so often my wife pops up with something I never suspected she'd say. I wonder, in this case, whether it is because men are generally the active ones, while women are passive. A women doesn't feel the need to *do* anything."

Afra herself states: "We sell what we have for what we need. Men their brains, women their bodies. Better than hypocrisy." Are we to believe that this comes from a top female scientist? Piers Anthony apparently expects us to.

In combining the Bene Gesserit, Afra, and Beatryx, we are back to the concept of womanhood presented in more traditional literature. I find it disastrous that these otherwise brilliant science fiction writers have neglected even to imagine a better lot for women, especially since they are so often the friends of other oppressed groups. Science fiction at its best points out short-comings in the present world; it has always been a powerful tool for the voice of social outrage. Apparently these men sense no outrage at women's position.

LETTER TO VIRGINIA WOOLF

How long have I, a woman, felt the need for a room of my own? I had one as a child and loved it. I wrote in it. I dreamed in it, I invented in it, I labored in it and I drew and painted in it. I was myself in it. I collected, hid and clutched my worldly goods in it and wallowed in its freedom like in nude midnight swimming. But marriage brought me company and I shared the bed so willingly and the house the same ... all ours, no more mine, until one day there was no place I felt alone and I salvaged an hour to loosen my thinking and swim metaphorically. Then I saw my husband craving a corner of his own to think and invent and grow. Seeing us together and separate at once I knew I needed a space all my own and so do we all. Even the dog has her corner! Ah, Virginia, you have told me nothing I did not already know.

Mary Yuill

MARGARET ATWOOD:
LOVE ON THE DARK SIDE OF THE MOON
by
Katherine E. Waters

In the popular media Margaret Atwood is often said to be writing about sexual politics. This concern is clear in her two novels where the exploitation of women by a variety of male lovers moves from satire to nightmare, and in some of the epigrams contained in her poetry. But in her work the sexual politics of the man-woman relationship is made complex by the fact that it is metaphor for, symptom and symbol of, bigger things.

Most obviously, sexual politics is a microcosm of the wider political reality of imperialism; and imperialism itself is a metaphor for the death of an organic universe where natural, human and spiritual 'run together' — a death brought about by cooperation between a political system (be it free enterprise or totalitarianism) and technology. Other writers, of course, Conrad, Lawrence, Forster in prose, Auden and Cummings in poetry, have used the personal as particularization of the socio-political, and the socio-political as metaphor for the universal. Atwood's distinction is that she does it from the viewpoint of feminine consciousness. Hence, the woman is often territory, the man often an american and emissary of technological progress. All this can be seen in a poem called "Backdrop Addresses Cowboy:"[1]

> Starspangled cowboy
> sauntering out of the almost-
> silly West, on your face
> a porcelain grin,
> tugging a papier-mâché cactus
> on wheels behind you with a string.
>
> you are innocent as a bathtub
> full of bullets.

Your righteous eyes, your laconic
trigger-fingers
people the streets with villains:
as you move, the air in front of you
blossoms with targets

and you leave behind you a heroic
trail of desolation:
beer bottles
slaughtered by the side
of the road, bird-
skulls bleaching in the sunset.

I ought to be watching
from behind a cliff or a cardboard storefront
when the shooting starts, hands clasped
in admiration,

but I am elsewhere.

Then what about me

what about the I
confronting you on that border
you are always trying to cross?

I am the horizon
you ride towards, the thing you can never lasso

I am also what surrounds you:
my brain
scattered with your
tincans, bones, empty shells,
the litter of your invasions.

I am the space you desecrate
as you pass through.

"Desecrate", the emphatically placed word of the climactic
line, emphasizes the "backdrop" as being not only the woman,
but also the land and the spiritual life of the universe.

That the cowboy in this poem is more than the-
oppressor-as-male, is reinforced by a poem called "At the Tourist
Centre in Boston", where Canada as a political and natural entity,
together with the woman and the man, are exploited:

There is my country under glass,
a white relief —
map with red dots for the cities,
reduced to the size of a wall

103

look here, Saskatchewan
is a flat lake, some convenient rocks
where two children pose with a father
and the mother is cooking something
in immaculate slacks by a smokeless fire,
her teeth white as detergent.

Whose dream is this, I would like to know:
is this a manufactured
hallucination, a cynical fiction, a lure
for export only?

I seem to remember people,
at least in the cities, also slush,
machines and assorted garbage.[2]

The "cynical fiction" is the technological cover-up of the "desecrated space," the travesty of purification in the manipulated, drycleaned family, the parody tribute to the organic in the deodorized fire-offering (note the mysterious "something"). One feels, not the overt presence but the pressure, of a female sensibility which has again and again been offered the "cynical fictions" of exploitation disguised as a pedestal.

Another complication in Atwood's work is that sexual politics is not only exploitation by males. It is often a man-woman battle in which her renunciations are as much a form of power politics as his demands, in which, through atrophy of feeling and language, things masquerade as their opposites: barbarism as civilization, power as love, victory as defeat. The protagonist of *Surfacing* says: "Saving the world, everyone wants to: men think they can do it with guns, women with their bodies, love conquers all, conquerors love all, mirages raised by words."[3] And the final insight of the apparently victimized Marion in *The Edible Woman* is that she may well be implicated in the cannibalism from which she was trying to escape: "Florence Nightingale was a cannibal."[4]

Sometimes this expresses itself through an awareness that is nearly predatory:

Which of us will survive
Which of us will survive the other[5]

Elsewhere it is expressed with sophisticated psychological and artistic awareness of civilized and verbal deceptions:

We are hard on each other
and call it honesty,
choosing our jagged truths

with care and aiming them across
the neutral table.

The things we say are
true; it is our crooked
aims, our choices
turn them criminal.
    ... If I love you
is that a fact or a weapon?[6]

Reinforcing the man-woman battle is the fact that the woman
speaker is often the artist and the "man" becomes her intractable
antagonist — human nature, society, language — which she must
use and which in turn wants to use her for its own ends; their
relationship dramatises the art-life relationship:

You held out your hand
I took your fingerprints

You asked for love
I gave you only descriptions

Please die I said
so I can write about it

But sometimes the male figure, presented as "camera man"
or engineer (both forms of the gunman), dramatises an art which
brutalizes life, shatters coherence, without recreating new life.
So the perspective shifts from the woman-as-artist to the woman-
as-average-human: "You ... with your camera and your spear."
Ultimately, then, the man-woman tension in Margaret
Atwood's poetry dramatises opposing aspects of herself. The
male-female confrontation is that of head and body, of predator
and victim, of history and ecology, of barbaric civilization and
Edenic centre; of conscious and unconscious, of fixed ego/role-
player and fluid, elusive "I." Rather than harmonizing into
"whole man alive," they remain disturbingly unresolved, or shattered by the violence of their encounter, or frozen by its emptiness.
An early poem, "Playing Cards," brings this out in reiterated
and intensifying images of dualism, alienation, inability to make
association and thus inability to make distinctions:

In this room we are always in:

tired with all the other games
we get out cards and play
at double
solitaire:
the only thing
either of us might win.

There's a queen.
Or rather two of them
joined at the waist, or near
(you can't tell where
exactly, under the thick
brocaded costume)
or is it one
woman with two heads?
Each has hair drawn back
made of lines
and a half-smile that is part
of a set pattern.

Each holds a golden flower
with five petals, ordered
and unwilting.

Outside there is a lake
or this time is it a street

There's a king (or kings)
too, with a beard to show
he is a man
and something abstract
in his hand
that might be either
a sceptre or a sword.

The colour doesn't matter,
black or red:
there's little choice between
heart and spade.
The important things
are the flowers and the swords;
but they stay flat,
are cardboard.

Outside there is a truck
or possibly a motorboat

and in this lighted room
across the table, we
confront each other

wearing no costumes.

You have nothing
that serves the function of a sceptre
and I have
certainly
no flowers.[8]

106

This poem introduces one of Atwood's most frequent and arresting male images: man as a fallen hero, embodying the fall of the spiritual, the historical and rational — the modern experience, presented through a female sensibility. Here is a curious passage in *Surfacing,* between the woman narrator and the other couple who at various times accuse her of hating men:

> I said "I think men ought to be superior." But neither of them heard the actual words; Anna looked at me as though I'd betrayed her and said "Wow, are you ever brainwashed," and David said "Want a job?"[9]

First, the loss of attraction and awe toward the man expresses the individual's loss of the numinous, and hence of the ability for self-transcendence. Margaret Atwood accepts this fallen divinity, skewers any false claims to it, yet is still honest enough to emotionally regret the loss, using the ironic feminist perspective to control the regret:

> It would be so good if you'd
> only stay up there
> where I put you
> I could believe you'd solve most of my religious problems
> You have to admit it's easier
> when you're somewhere else.[10]

Trust, action, reverence for the irrational, are difficult without gods. Her ambivalence is seen in two recent poems, "They Eat Out"[11] and "After the Agony."[12]

> In restaurants we argue
> over which of us will pay for your funeral
>
> though the real question is
> whether or not I will make you immortal.
>
> At the moment only I
> can do it and so
>
> I raise the magic fork
> over the plate of beef fried rice
>
> and plunge it into your heart.
> There is a faint pop, a sizzle
>
> and through your own split head
> you rise up glowing;
>
> the ceiling opens
> a voice sings Love Is A Many

Splendoured Thing
you hang suspended above the city

in blue tights and a red cape,
your eyes flashing in unison

The other diners regard you
some with awe, some only with boredom:

they cannot decide if you are a new weapon
or only a new advertisement.

As for me, I continue eating;
I liked you better the way you were,
but you were always ambitious.

* * *

After the agony in the guest
bedroom, you lying by the
overturned bed
your face uplifted, neck propped
against the windowsill, my arm
under you, cold moon
shining down through the window

wine mist rising
around you, an almost-
visible halo

You say, Do you
love me, do you love me

I answer you:
I stretch your arms out
one to either side,
your head slumps forward.

Later I take you home
in a taxi, and you
are sick in the bathtub.

In the first poem the deification through power is ridiculed, both by its description and by the attitudes of the other diners and of the speaker. Yet the irony falls as well on the bored diners, for whom the skygods of the west have become cartoon figures, weapons with built-in obsolescence, or disembodied flying men armed with the newest household cleanser; for whom life without the numinous remains merely a cannibalistic consumerism instead of a communion — "having long forgotten the difference between an annunciation and a parking ticket."[13]

In the second poem the deification through love is denied. The man, here the sacrificial Dionysius ("wine mist")/Christ ("agony in the . . .," "halo," "arms out to either side") figure, is not reborn in transcendence. But if he is no longer a miracle, she is no longer a miracle-worker, for myths are made by human beings as a way of resolving the paradoxes of their nature. His failure is hers too.

Inability to change *him* embodies limitations on changing herself:

I can change my-
self more easily
than I can change you

I could grow bark and
become a shrub

or switch back in time
to the woman image left
in a cave rubble, the drowned
stomach bulbed with fertility,
face a tiny bead, a
lump, queen of the termites

or (better) speed myself up,
disguise myself in the knuckles
and purple-veined veil of old ladies . . .[14]

The only available metamorphoses are downward in form and time; in a world without gods or illusions of gods, the images of one's final destiny are of death without rebirth, "dead roots bleaching in the swamps."[15]

This loss is connected with the lack of ecstasy, of transcendence in a sex, a feature of Atwood's poetry. This connection could be seen in "Playing Cards" in the inoperative "sceptre" and "flower," symbols of both sacred and sexual vitality. As D. H. Lawrence saw, this is the price to be paid when the numinous is lost. In Atwood's poetry we are beyond considering whether or not the price *should* be paid; rather, we enter the experience of one who *is* paying the price:

What do you expect after this?
Applause? Your name on stone?

You will have nothing
but me and in a worse way than before.[16]

The fallen male figure dramatises also the loss of cultural identity in the form of history which in so much traditional literature is bound up with the male's quest for the father/leader/hero, the woman's quest for such cultural identity through the mediating figure of the husband/lover/teacher, is given a devastating metaphor in a quiet, but lethal poem, "The Green Man: for the Boston Strangler:"[17]

The green man, before whom
the doors melted,

the window man, the furnace man, the electric
light man,
the necessary man, always expected.

He said the right words,
they opened the doors;

He turned towards them
his face, a clear mirror
because he had no features.

In it they saw reflected their
own sanity;

They saw him as a function . . . .

The figure fallen is seen as "My beautiful wooden leader/with your heartful of medals/made of wood"[18] or, in the following poem, as an old man who has lost his power:

The old man with his
scarred heart clamped
between sheets, listening
for the sound of feathers descending
over his head

whose skilled hands once
cut flesh, shipped
horses through mounded
snow, sculpted
muscles, now carves

tiny birds with pins
in their backs. These
he sends to daughters, grand-
daughters bluejay, kingfisher

hummingbird, its wings outstretched
across my throat, wood
soul[19]

Yet perhaps the images sent to her show that she has really no more identity, no more freedom than when she was the direct

110

object of his power; no less pain, even less meaning to the pain, than before.

Ultimately, this male figure and the human history he embodies shrinks to darkness, as we see in "Projected Slide of an Unknown Soldier"[20] which begins with light overcoming darkness and ends with dark pushing out light at the individual, historical and linguistic level:

Upon the wall a face
uttered itself
in light, pushing
aside the wall's darkness;

Around it leaves, glossy,
perhaps tropical, not making
explicit whether the face was
breaking through them, wore them
as disguise, was crowned
with them or sent them
forth as rays,
a slippery halo;

The clothes were invisible,
the eyes
hidden; the nose
foreshortened: a muzzle.

Hair on the upper lip.
On the skin the light shone, wet
with heat; the teeth
of the open mouth reflected it
as absolute.

The mouth was open
stretched wide in a call or howl
(there was no tongue)
of agony, ultimate
command or simple famine.
The canine teeth ranged back
into the throat and vanished.

The mouth was filled with darkness.
The darkness in the open mouth
uttered in pushing
aside the light.

So for him, for her, for their world, the journey into history becomes "a journey into the skull;" the threat of strangulation becomes the threat of self-strangulation through drowning —

another frequent image in Atwood's poetry. However, darkness uttered in darkness is not entirely negative, as the design of St John's Last Gospel shows, and as we'll see in her poetry.

In representing the directing intelligence of history, the man figure embodies the rational, the linear, the ego — in short, the dominance of the visual. Thus, "light" is associated with him, and the emphasis is often on his eyes fixed on an object: the "cowboy," eyes fixed on the horizon, the "camera man" with his "glass eye" who wants to shoot his girl "composed ... in front of a church, for perspective,"[21] the "wooden leader" gazing afar, the purposeful pioneer husband of Susanna Moodie.

In representing the sort of life absurdly violated by history, the woman speaker renders the physical, emotional, unconscious personal life, an apprehension which is biological, geological and ecological — what Joan Didion has spoken of as

"all one's actual apprehension of what it is like to be a woman, the irreconcilable difference of it — that sense of living one's deepest life underwater, that dark involvement with blood and birth and death."[22]

The sense vehicle for this sort of awareness is the tactile — and Margaret Atwood joins other contemporary women poets such as Sylvia Plath and Anne Sexton in the intensity and predominance she gives to this sense which embodies a different experience of time, space and inner reality. (After all, her now famous epigram: "you fit into me/like a hook into an eye/a fish hook/an open eye"[23] assaults us primarily by a switch from the eye as visual to the eye as tactile).

This 'female' perspective is more appalling than the 'male' one: it is the chaos of non-perspective, of subject-object confusion, of loss of ego-self. Here is Susanna Moodie's awareness of her husband:

My husband walks in the frosted field
an X, a concept
defined against a blank;
he swerves, enters the forest
and is blotted out.[24]

But it is also more potentially creative: it is at least not a falsely secure 'arrangement' of reality; if it loses stable ego, it discovers a fluid potential self; if it loses context, it discovers a universe of potential form; if it loses history, it discovers pre-history and apocalypse. In short, it is the landscape of the modern artist.

112

In a passage from *Of a Fire on the Moon* Norman Mailer, calling himself "Aquarius," writes of the pictures taken of the dark side of the moon by the crew of Apollo 11, and is led to speculate on modern painting:

. . . nothing for hundreds of miles before the eyes but swellings and distensions of the terrain like a skin beneath which furies must have wrung themselves, a bewildering endlessly worked-over expanse almost without rays, a stretch of bumpy, knobby pockmarked upthrown churnings equal to the view from a low boat — without horizon, one could never sight a level, and direction was hopeless, a windtwisted choppy sea had been frozen on the instant to stone. So one had no sense of scale . . . . it took Aquarius close to thirty years to comprehend why Cezanne was the father of modern art and godfather to photographs of the far side of the moon . . . . Before Cezanne every surface was recognizable in its own right . . . . one could cut out a square inch of canvas, show it to an unfamiliar eye, and the response would be that it was a piece of lace, or a square of velvet, for the canvas had been painted to look exactly like lace or velvet.

Cezanne, however, had looked to destroy the surface. A tablecloth in any one of his still life, taken inch by square inch, resembled the snowfields of mountains; his apples could be the paint-stained walls of a barn, or the clay roundings of a rock; the trunks of his trees were stems, or pillars, or hairs beneath a microscope; . . . . the skin which ran from a man's eyes to the corner of his mouth was like the sun-beaten terrain of his hills. Something in that vision spoke like the voice of the century to come, something in his work turned other painters out of their own directions and into a search for the logic of the abstract.[25]

Here is a poem by Margaret Atwood, "A Soul Geologically," whose landscape resembles that of "the far side of the moon" and of Cezanne:

The longer we stay here the harder
it is for me to see you.

Your outline, skin
that marks you off
melts in this light

and from behind your face
the unknown areas appear:

hills, yellow-pelted, dried earth
bubbles, or thrust up
steeply as knees

the sky a flat blue desert,

these spaces you fill
with their own emptiness.

Your shape wavers, glares,
like heat above the road,

then you merge and extend:
you have gone,
in front of me there is a stone ridge.

Which of these forms
have you taken:

hill, tree clawed
to the rock, fallen rocks worn
and rounded by the wind

you are the wind,
you contain me

I walk in the white silences
of your mind, remembering

the way it is millions of years before
on the wide floor of the sea

while my eyes lift like continents
to the sun and erode slowly.[26]

Here the surface and context of a human being (again, the "man", associated with linear-visual, with light and with ego ("face") is destroyed and occupies any of the possible forms in the universe, in a "female" vision that is both bewildering and consciousness-expanding, both humanly desolate and imaginatively creative.

In Margaret Atwood's poetry, then, the man-woman relationship is symptom and symbol of the unsolved riddles of her humanity. But ultimately the man-woman relationship is also subject and raison d'être for almost all her poetry. Her poetry is love poetry, though its affirmations find no adequate social or religious structure — rather they express themselves poetically, in resolved images, in rhythms which can open out to convey renewal, in shifts of tone. In most of her volumes of poetry, the poems are arranged so that they begin with alienation, end with partial reconciliation through the image of a man-woman relationship which "does not move like love,"[27] as we conventionally think of love.

Atwood's most recent volume, *Power Politics,* is her most terrible rendering of the past and present cruelties in the man-woman relationship. It is also a commitment to a new man-woman relationship if we are to survive and if we are to start at last to become human. Unlike preachers and politicians, Atwood the poet does not present answers and programs; rather she raises questions, and, through words arranged in poems, she gives us moments in which (possibly) we may begin to feel and to transform feeling into a new consciousness.

Perhaps we begin by rejecting the disguised power roles springing from sex role socialization: leader/lover for man, nurse/lover for woman; these roles have degenerated respectively to "policeman" and "used angel." But to choose to "own oneself" is to choose the even greater pain of reality, move closer to the reality of death:

> If you deny these uniforms
> and choose to repossess
> yourself, your future
> will be less dignified, more painful, death will be sooner,
> (it is no longer possible
> to be both human and alive): lying piled with
> the others, your face and body
> covered so thickly with scars
> only the eyes show through.[28]

No structure to make pain and death meaningful is suggested. Nevertheless, the "eyes" persist to seek it. Masochistic delight in self-pain (such as one finds, for example, in Sylvia Plath) is avoided.

Rejecting these "uniforms" of sex roles, one ends up with a very different centerfold man or woman:

> They were all inaccurate:
>
> the hinged bronze man, the fragile man
> built of glass pebbles,
> the fanged man with his opulent capes and boots
>
> peeling away from you in scales.
>
> It was my fault but you helped,
> you enjoyed it.
>
> Neither of us will enjoy
> the rest: you following me
>
> down streets, hallways, melting
> when I touch you,
> avoiding the sleeves of the bargains
> I hold out for you,
> your face corroded by truth,

crippled, persistent. You ask
like the wind, again and again and
wordlessly, for the one forbidden thing:

love without mirrors and not for
my reasons but your own.[29]

Yet this truthful man and woman, unmasked, still seek love and
power — after all, we don't know yet what we'll find when
we throw away the sex-roles. By asking for "the one forbidden
thing," perhaps she suggests once more that, as with the fruit
of the forbidden tree, directing one's own destiny and discovering
that destiny to be death, go together; so perhaps the "thing"
asked for can never quite be granted: "human kind cannot bear
very much reality," Eliot wrote. Though we (probably) will and
should reject our present social roles, other roles, other games
will probably succeed them, though we cannot imagine their forms.

At the center, then, one is not likely to find unfallen man.
Although Margaret Atwood might say, along with Stephen
Dedalus, "History is a nightmare from which I am trying to
awake," she refuses the temptations of the flight from history.
Walking along "84th Street, Edmonton"[30]

The pain in my fingers is
the only thing that's real, the houses,
trees, parked cars are
a tight surface covering
panic or only more
nothing than I've ever seen

I could stop. This could be where
I stop finally. I could
disappear, say
at the next driveway; but
courage, genesis descends
here also or never

I will build a history
in the backyard from solid
rocks, populate it
with dried sticks and the old newspaper-
faced gods

covered by twilight and the first
white snow.

In the "solid rocks" we see the strength-in-vulnerability she
gains from observing the way life works in nature to withstand
corrosive truth:

Beyond truth,
tenacity: of those
dwarf trees & mosses,
hooked into straight rock
believing the sun's lies & thus
refuting/gravity

& of this cactus, gathering
itself together
against the sand, yes tough
rind & spikes but doing
the best it can[31]

The barrenness of nature becomes a positive element; for it
is a miraculous fact that life grows in the stoniest ground and
that indeed such dwarf plants are the likeliest to survive large-scale
devastation. These wintry stripped-down settings, metaphors for
a demilitarized zone between hope and hopelessness, are where
the always-central man and woman find themselves when they
have "put down the target," the map with "vulnerable sections
marked in red" of each other:

See, we are alone in
the dormant field, the snow
that cannot be eaten or captured

Here there are no armies
here there is no money

It is cold and getting colder

We need each others'
breathing, warmth, surviving
is the only war we can afford, stay

walking with me, there is almost
time/if we can only
make it as far as

the (possibly) last summer[32]

In the last three passages cited above we see another of her
"strategies" for survival: the joining of the natural cycle to the
human, to recreate our era as *pre*-historic, *pre*-human. For along
with a number of other women in literature — D. H. Lawrence's
Ursula Brangwen, Doris Lessing's Martha Quest, Margaret
Atwood's speaker feels that we have not yet become human in
that we have not yet got beyond the stage of political animals
wielding love as a weapon rather than bearing it as a gift.

117

Marriage is not
a house or even a tent

it is before that, and colder:

the edge of the forest, the edge
of the desert

                    the unpainted stairs
at the back where we squat
outside, eating popcorn

the edge of the receding glacier
where painfully and with wonder
at having survived even
this far
we are learning to make fire[33]

The female biological experience of carrying the life-to-come,
of its changing forms, of its long gestation would seem to help
her create and accept such a vision. In the final poem of her
last volume, ''He is last Seen,''[34] the man figure, walking towards
her carrying ''a new death'' becomes a gift-bearer and then
merges into the first human being born

through the weeks and months, across
the rocks, up from
the pits and starless
deep nights of the sea

towards firm ground and safety.

Notes

1. Margaret Atwood, *The Animals in That Country,* Oxford University Press, Toronto, 1968, pp. 50-51.
2. *Ibid.,* p. 18.
3. Margaret Atwood, *Surfacing,* McClelland & Stewart, Toronto, 1972, pp. 162-3.
4. Margaret Atwood, *The Edible Woman,* McClelland & Stewart, Toronto, 1969, p. 263.
5. Margaret Atwood, *Power Politics,* Anansi, Toronto, 1971, p. 23.
6. *Ibid.,* pp. 24-25.
7. *Ibid.,* p. 10.
8. Margaret Atwood, *The Circle Game,* Anansi, Toronto, 1967, pp. 24-25.
9. *Surfacing,* p. 111.
10. *Power Politics,* p. 21.
11. *Ibid.,* p. 5.
12. *Ibid.,* p. 6.

13. *Ibid.,* p. 30.
14. *Ibid.,* p. 4.
15. *The Circle Game,* p. 60.
16. *Power Politics,* p. 20.
17. *Animals,* p. 12.
18. *Power Politics,* p. 7.
19. Margaret Atwood, *Procedures for Underground,* Oxford University Press, Toronto, 1970, p. 11.
20. *Ibid.,* p. 46.
21. *The Circle Game,* p. 45.
22. Joan Didion, *The New York Times Book Review,* July 30, 1972, p. 14.
23. *Power Politics,* p. 1.
24. Margaret Atwood, *The Journals of Susanna Moodie,* Oxford University Press, 1970, p. 19.
25. Norman Mailer, *Of a Fire on the Moon,* Little, Brown, Boston, 1970, pp. 300-301.
26. *Procedures,* p. 58.
27. *Power Politics,* p. 46.
28. *Ibid.,* p. 30.
29. *Ibid.,* p. 55.
30. *Procedures,* pp. 52-53.
31. *Power Politics,* p. 36.
32. *Ibid.,* pp. 37-38.
33. *Procedures.,* p. 60.
34. *Power Politics,* p. 56.

FEMINIST POETRY

The masculine Pope
decided the hemlines for the new convent would be
one and a half inches above the knee, my dear, what will
Mr. Adams think of me, and the Pope gave strict orders that
we also read one book from The Book of the Month Club to keep
up with the times,
Sister Louisa, i am not attacking the Pope
(it is quite wrong, i know)
well if i leave
And ask a man for a match
And have 2 babies instead of 23
And become President of the United States
he, he will damn me personnally, and if i don't look
like the girl with the freshest mouth in town my husband
won't let me take holy communion and when i'm 55 he will
put his daughter in our bed who is 21; the only time a lady
is a human being
is (excuse me reader but i cannot
find the words to express myself)

mary melfi

just
  because
      i wore pants
    they said
  i was not a woman underneath my pants
          because
        they could not believe a woman was more
than a dress of the latest fashion;
        to all of them i say: yes
            i am a pair of nylon stockings,
          but also
            i am a mother of 4 children,
          i am a janitor, like most men
        wash their cars instead,
            i am a schoolteacher, like
        most men are only a small part of the
                day,
          i am mind, reading Plato inbetween
        McCall,
            and who are you, mankind?
        and of course i know
            you are my partner in
        the night, and i thank-you for
          my happiness during our
              peace.

mary melfi

WHITE KISS OF LIGHTNING

Bleak stretch of wet sand
cold
numbing these barefeet
padding slowly at melancholy's pace
among shivering starfish;
White Kiss of Lightning,
icy sliver through this burning body—
feverish and trembling,
lit cruelly by his torch of comprehension.
Dry wood, petrified from ages, ages of isolation
sputters and gasps in pain;
only to be extinguished by a huge kindness —
the salty wave and biting wind —
ecstatic freedom shared with the soaring seagull
under my true father, the immensity of firmament.
Then the long flowing hair no longer whips my face
and transcends the laugh,
but hides the aching soul from the prison
into which I am mercilessly thrown;
and when I turn, I find
that there is no Window.

Margit Boronkay

LETTER TO MY MOTHER:

Anatomy, mother, is not destiny, and Freud's mathematics are all wrong. A Pavlovian technique seems to have manipulated women into becoming puppets in the hands of capitalist perpetrators of ''feminine accessories'' (vaginal sprays, make-up, fashion gimmicks, ad nauseum). But no, mother, women are not lacking what men have, nor are they sex objects to enhance and honor male anatomy. Freud, you must remember, was born of woman's flesh and had *her* vagina not been, *he* could not have called her a castrated male.

I wrote this poem for you

M adonna of my flesh
O varies and breasts
T ouch my mind and
H old my trembling fears.
E mbrace me,
R avaged woman, mother

Mary Sachla

    i
        want for awhile again
            The man
    and then,
            i will, if it pleases me,
        tear the individual's face
                into a ball of memory,
                    — in the morning sun.

mary melfi

124

POEM BY ZELDA

found by

Elspeth Buitenhuis

When I like women I want to own them, to dominate them, to have them admire me.

F. Scott Fitzgerald, Notebooks

I want you to stop writing fiction.

F. Scott Fitzgerald, to Zelda

To read Milford's biography, *Zelda,* [1] is to see F. Scott Fitzgerald's deliberate thwarting of whatever talents Zelda possessed, or, rather, the channelling of those talents into areas which did not threaten his success. At the same time, he had no qualms about ransacking her letters and diaries for material for his own books. This attitude almost certainly contributed to Zelda's mental breakdown and quite possibly deprived us of a great woman novelist.

I am no poet, but for sometime I have been appalled at the revelation of F. Scott Fitzgerald's control of what might have been a creativity more fertile than his own. Thus this found poem:

Darling, Sweet D.O. —
I have often told you
that I am that little fish
who swims about
under
a shark
and, I believe,
lives indelicately on its offal.
Life moves over me in a
vast
black
shadow
and I swallow whatever it drops with relish,

having learned in a very hard school
that one cannot be
both a parasite
and enjoy self-nourishment
without moving in worlds
too fantastic for even my disordered imagination
to people with meaning.
Goofo —
I adore you
and worship you
and I am very miserable that you be made
even temporarily
unhappy
by those divergencies in direction
in myself
which I cannot satisfactorily explain
and which leave me eternally alone
except for you
and
baffled.

1. Nancy Milford, *Zelda,* Avon Books, New York, 1970, p. 304.

WOMEN
AND THEIR BODIES

a big hole,
   sits in my body,
     soon ready,
     to become me, entirely.

mary melfi

THE QUESTION OF CHILDREN

OPPOSITION TO BIRTH CONTROL

by

Lise Fortier, M.D., F.R.C.S.(C)

Physicians, during many years, fought contraception with ferocity. To the end of the 19th century, in England, although high maternal and infantile morbidity and mortality were worrying the medical profession and although morbidity and mortality were often related to a non-controlled fertility, the medical profession, during more than forty years, tried to ignore the causes of the problem.

Around 1860, ignorance, becoming impossible, was replaced by a violent opposition. Lord Amberley, the father of Bertrand Russell, was accused of having scandalously insulted the medical profession when he suggested that it should interest itself in contraception. In 1887, a physician named Albutt was expelled from the medical society because he had published a textbook in which there was a chapter on contraception. During that time the word contraception was never printed without a series of adjectives such as "egoist", "immoral", "lustful"; it was claimed that contraception caused cancer, sterility, nymphomania, suicide and amnesia. On the other hand it was easy to deduce, from the size of their families, that physicians were the first ones to practise birth control. As recently as 1905, the British Medical Association condemned the use of contraceptives.

It was only after the First World War that, slowly and reluctantly, physicians began to change their views. The availibility of oral contraceptives for which medical prescription was needed and also the orientation of medicine towards preventing rather than curing, forced physicians to adopt a new position.

Religious and sexual taboos explain those attitudes and they have not disappeared with the Victorian Age. As an example of this, everybody still discusses family planning which implies that only persons who are legally or religiously made up as a

131

family can use contraception. In reality, under a non-compromising term such as family planning we are discussing birth planning and in a broader sense still, contraception. All family planning implies contraception, but all contraception is not necessarily family planning. Thus, the prostitutes need contraception but it would be hypocrisy to call this family planning; the same applies to teens experimenting with sexuality or to the couple which, without any desire to procreate, lives temporarily in common law.

This euphemism reflects a reluctance to accept the idea of contraception, reluctance that physicians have shown as much as other people. In fact, this reluctance turns out to be a frank opposition when sterilization and abortion are concerned. One of the main objections of hospitals to liberalized abortion and sterilization is that they will do only those two kinds of operations, and consequently they won't be able to train skilled obstetricians and gynaecologists.

But about ten years ago, when reliable means of contraception were still not widely available, nobody was complaining because residents in obstetrics and gynecology spent at least a third of their time doing D&C for incomplete abortions (most often illegal abortions) or watching over normal deliveries. As long as it was nature (as they then believed) and not women who were forcing them to do it, physicians had no objection to being only technicians.

There is still a lot of opposition to contraception which, in my opinion, is not church-centered but male-centered. After all, medicine is a man's world until recently forbidden to females, and physicians, by becoming physicians, did not rid themselves of their prejudices as males and of their overlasting desire to dominate females. Through law, religion, economy, traditions, all human rights now recognized as fundamental, the right to vote, the right to own property, the right to be educated, the right to self-determination were denied to women. When this attitude became very difficult to justify, men have unwillingly granted those rights, in theory, although in reality it still seems that we are living with double-standards.

Freud has described the envy of the penis as an essential component of the feminine psychology. To be sure in the victorian age which was his, the golden age of the double-standard, when everything was permitted to man and everything forbidden to women, a sensible woman could not but realize what privileges the ownership of a penis could bring and, by deduction, desire
132

one. Freud and many of his followers came to the point where they considered woman as an incomplete being, one without a penis. Surprisingly they never saw men as a being without a uterus! The functioning of such an incomplete being could not possibly be normal so it had to be modified.

From this came what I call the "delirium of the vaginal orgasm." Contrary to the most elementary common sense, which shows the clitoris as being the physiologic counterpart of the penis and, as such, the seat of the orgasm, man wanting to believe that the mere fact of introducing his penis in the vagina of the woman, should give her great ecstasies, has invented that in women, orgasm must be transferred from the clitoris to the vagina. Nobody would have ever thought of asking men to transfer the orgasm from the penis to the scrotum. But for women to do such (if one thinks of the natural insensitivity of the vagina, in which a foreign body can be introduced and as soon forgotten) was considered quite normal.

In the same order of thinking, one cannot escape comparing the flightiness with which thousand of ovaries were removed for the tenuous of reasons, while everybody was treating testes with the outmost respect, not permitting them to be suppressed unless under a threat of death. A psychiatrist once asked me to sterilize a young woman whose suicidal tendencies were apparent, in his opinion, only during her premenstrual period. It wouldn't have crossed his mind to castrate a man because the same tendencies have shown themselves after an ejaculation.

In the same way, male and female attitudes toward sterilization are so far apart that you would think only one of them derives advantages from it. Men shun sterilization; women beg for it, even when their reason for doing so has nothing to do with them. They will beg for it because their husband is alcoholic, epileptic, has a heart disease or a nervous breakdown or simply to make sex more enjoyable to their male partners. A man whose wife has had six pregnancies, two miscarriages, two curettages, a phlebitis, has taken pills for six years and has varicose veins, still thinks she should be the one to submit to sterilization.

After all, she is used to general anaesthesia and operative procedures; why make a fuss about one more? Even when you have explained to some women how much more complicated it is to sterilize them compared with men, that it implies a hospital stay, major surgery and a convalescence, they will insist on having it done on themselves; their poor male darlings are so afraid of needles and live in the fear of becoming eunuchs should we

133

tamper with their genitals. But male patients are not the only ones responsible for this attitude. Male physicians, probably sensing that they could be male patients, are doing their best to discourage their like from getting sterilized by frightening them with predictions or improbable complications.

With this as a background it seems interesting to look at a rule of accreditation for hospitals, whereby one must consult if there is to be an operation resulting in the sterilization of a woman when this woman is still in the reproductive age, whatever the reason for this intervention may be. Was this brought about by the abuse of unscrupulous physicians who had been practising hysterectomies, as a quick way to fortune? If so, why is it still asked for women who have cancer and why is it not asked after women have passed the age of reproduction? Or why is it not asked in case of tonsilectomy or appendectomy, to take as an example two kinds of operation which were done without rime or reason?

For those two operations, it seems that a tissue committee is sufficient. There is no need for consultation prior to a craniotomy or a gastrectomy. Does this mean that the reproductive function of a woman is more important in the eyes of physicians than her life? A woman shouldn't be deprived of this function except for very serious reasons; she must not escape pregnancy. That certain women have begged for hysterectomy, to put an end to their undesired pregnancies, does not justify this rule. It only underlines that physicians were not fulfilling their obligations to offer alternatives, that they were not fulfilling their obligations to protect the mental and physical health of women. That to the control of the tissue committee one must add a mandatory consultation with another gynaecologist, only falsifies the object of the consultation; nowadays, this consultation is most often a matter of complacency, no matter that it comes from somebody in whom we have total confidence or be it that it would bother us to object to a decision unless this decision is too evidently a mistake.

A consultation shouldn't be a way to control the doings of a physician, but rather a way to enlighten him and to help him make a decision. Consultation is also mandatory in case of caesarean section. I have known a time when everything was tried, short of killing the mother, rather than section her, so that she would come to the caesarean section almost moribund. In view of this, the consultation for section seems to me a bad joke. One wonders from where all these precautions emerged when one knows that

134

the great causes of maternal mortality — haemorrhages, toxemia, infection — have in great part been controlled by this caesarean section, so benign that it can be compared to a normal delivery. Is it that one looks with suspicion on everything that permits a woman to free herself from the danger and the pain of having a child?

Before hastening to refute this seemingly ridiculous hypothesis, think of the great scandal brought upon by the use of anaesthesia in obstetrics, because woman was meant to give birth in pain. When women decided to get rid of this attitude, somebody found a way to bring them back where they were before the discovery of anaesthesia; they were simply convinced that they would be better mothers if they were to deliver without anaesthesia. Anaesthesia and analgesia being dispensed in any other condition causing pain or in any other operation, it was rather embarrassing to refuse it in obstetrics. There are dangers to anaesthesia, dangers for the mother (it is still an important cause of maternal death when given by unskilled personnel, but this only emphasizes the dangers of pregnancy) and dangers for the infant. But while in any other operation the dangers are being accepted as an unevitable part of the fight against pain, in obstetrics, it was considered that one could do without anesthesia for the benefit of the child.

This is a worthy end, but women were never asked their opinion on the subject, everything being decided by the male physicians. For many years it was considered normal always to sacrifice the mother for the child even when her life was concerned. It went a step further: physicians tried to convince women that they would be superior females and superior mothers should they do completely without anaesthesia. This new theory called natural childbirth brought women back exactly where they were before the discovery of anaesthesia. One wonders why such attention has been given to surgical anaesthesia which, after all, somebody may never have experienced in his lifetime while the relief of obstetrical pains which are the fate of most women, and repeatedly so, has not evoked much attention. I am convinced that if man had been the one to deliver babies and suffer from it, research in this area would have long ago produced a safe and easy way to relieve it.

Another way of acting which reflects the same philosophy is the one by which physicians have tried to convince women that pregnancy is a normal situation — desirable, physiologically and socially, and that not to become pregnant is a failure — keeping silent about the real dangers of pregnancy the mortality rate of which was around 45 by 1,000 and did not drop until, from the knowledge of the important changes produced in the organism by pregnancy, physicians treated it as a disease demanding intensive care.

Obstetricians, in particular, have had an interest in defining pregnancy as the state of health most desirable for a woman. Whenever I point out to other physicians that the maternal mortality dropped only when they started treating pregnancy as a disease, even the most broadminded ones jump and tell me that, after all, pregnancy is a normal function of the organism. Certainly it is a function; and if normal means that it is shared by most, certainly it is a normal function. But to say that it is normal in the sense that, like other functions, it helps to maintain the health of the organism, I disagree. I do not say that pregnancy is a disease because I am not sure what a disease is or how to define it, if not by defining health.

Those two terms have been the subject of much controversy by minds better equipped than mine to deal with philosophy and semantics. But whatever definition you turn to, it boils down to a departure from the state of health or an abnormal state of the body as a whole. It can be said to manifest itself subjectively by abnormal sensations essentially unpleasant, worrying or painful. In human medicine it is a group of abnormal phenomenona, physical or psychological having one or many causes, endogenous or exogenous, generally but not necessarily known, and which can be accompanied by by pathologic manifestations functional, biochemical or morphological.

If disease is an alteration of health, what is health? The most accepted, but still very controversial definition is the one of the World Health Organization, which defines health, not only as an absence of disease of physical disability, but as a mental, physical and social feeling of well-being. How does this apply to pregnancy? Certainly, from the beginning in many subjects there has been a series of abnormal sensations or symptoms essentially unpleasant, worrying or painful. To enumerate a few: nausea, vomiting, sleepyness, tiredness, constipation, shortness of breath, striae gravidarum, eodema, backache. It climaxes in the delivery with all the pains, the bleeding, the tears that accompany it and, furthermore, as late complications, prolapse, cystocele and rectocele.

Also, what could be considered in this enumeration are the specific complications of pregnancy such as miscarriage, placenta praevia, abruptic placentae, toxemia or the multiple complications of labour which demand delivery by caesarean section, or post-partum psychosis or the fact that many serious diseases are aggravated by pregnancy. As time goes on, and the pregnancies are more numerous, the risk to the health of the mother gets to be greater and greater, so that by the tenth birth the mortality rate is five times the usual one. Of 29 maternal deaths in the state of Missouri in 1968, twelve happened in women who had had more than five pregnancies and those findings are the same everywhere. The maternal deaths, which are directly related to complications secondary to great multiparity, would be very much reduced if contraception was used.

So pregnancy is not supposed to be a disease. Yet, I don't know how to define a state which brings about so many unpleasant symptoms and so many dreadful complications. I know of no other function in the human being which is so threatening for the individual. A woman who asks for an abortion or a sterilization feels that way, feels that the pregnancy is threatening her well-being, maybe her physical well-being but, most often, her psychological and social well-being. As a woman I have been more attuned to this feeling than many of my male colleagues could ever be, because they cannot feel as threatened as a woman can be by pregnancy and they can not identify themselves as closely with the patient.

Our society considers it the right of everybody to protect himself from serious threats. Physicians, although they knew that it was medically indicated, have been indifferent or definitely hostile to contraception and to abortion. As a rule, the medical profession is made up of conservative and conformist beings. It does not include many intellectuals or many revolutionaries; it is mostly composed of technicians. Our intellectual evolution is not made under the push of internal conviction but by the pressure of public opinion.

As an example, may I quote the absence of a statement by the profession on the hygiene and safety of the worker before the unions imposed their own policy on the subject. Also, let us remember that the American Medical Association once opposed obligatory vaccination against smallpox, the establishment of blood banks, the intervention of the federal government for the construction and founding of medical faculties and help to students, that it opposed government subsidies to reduce maternal and infantile mortality and any form of social security. Physicians have left medical philosophy to be elaborated by people outside of medicine. I think it is time that they look after their own thoughts, that they dissociate themselves from a philosophy and a morality which aims to subject women to their biological destiny, by law if needed, as it is done in many countries.

A very good gynaecologist, consulted on what to be done about a patient who, without any known pathology, had had nine successive miscarriages, more complicated each time and needing more and more blood transfusions, refused to sterilize her. To those who objected, because of the dangers incurred by the patient, he answered: ''What can we do, it is the destiny of women!''

This attitude of resignation faced with destiny is contrary to the raison d'être of medicine which is to help people fight an illfated biological destiny. As gynaecologists, we are committed to see that every woman who ventures into pregnancy does so of her own free will, with a realistic knowledge of the danger inherent in the situation and with the possibilities of defending herself against them so that every birth turns out to be a desired and happy event.

PREGNANCY AND CHILDBIRTH

by

Shirley L. P. Gardiner

The recent experience of a pregnancy and childbirth was the motivating factor in my deciding to present an analysis of the evaluations of pregnancy and childbirth made by a number of women. Altogether, I collected data from twenty-two women. Since the number is rather small, I do not intend to draw any profound conclusions, but rather wish this to be regarded as a pilot study from which a longer, more in-depth study could be initiated. Most of the women in my study are middle class women. Some are working class women. None are poor. I believe the content would have been considerably different had I been able to contact third world women. My main reason for not attempting this is that I think they are already hassled and I felt it would have been presumptuous of me to impose upon their time for this type of study. Should a more in-depth study be done, it would be imperative that poor women and lower working class women be contacted.

I intend to devote the latter part of this paper to a brief analysis of the literature most frequently read by expectant mothers.

The first section of my questionnaire or interview dealt with the subject herself. I was interested to know whether or not she felt that the pregnancy, or enjoyment of it, was affected by whether or not the pregnancy was a planned one. Here it is interesting to note that those women who had pregnancies before the 'Pill', and who had unplanned pregnancies, did not feel that the pregnancy or enjoyment of it was affected in any way by the fact that it was unplanned. They seemed to accept this occurrence as part of life, God's will, and made the best of it. Those who have had pregnancies in the past ten years felt that the pregnancy if unplanned was definitely affected, in that they had little enjoyment of it in the first months, though they adjusted to it in the latter part of the pregnancy and did manage to reap some enjoyment from the fact. A few had seriously contemplated abortion, but because of the difficulty of securing one or because of guilt feelings, did not seek one, and said that they also, in the latter part of the pregnancy, came to look forward to the birth of the child, though they still had feelings of resentment, not towards the child, but towards the 'system', which they felt had imposed this experience upon them.

All of the women that I contacted had either a husband or a boyfriend with them throughout the pregnancy, and about eighty per cent also had their husbands or boyfriends with them during labour. Those who did not have their husbands with them during labour were women who had their pregnancies 20-25 years ago. When I asked whether or not they felt that this was important, all but one of those women who had recent pregnancies said that indeed it was important. No matter how well prepared they felt they were, it was good to have support from someone who cared emotionally. Most felt that the hospital was a cold alienating place and having a person who was emotionally involved was reassuring. ''There are times when you need someone to support you, to help you stand by your decisions when you weaken, to rub your back and help you turn while you're in labour, to heighten the most beautiful experience in life by sharing it.''

For those who had their babies by natural childbirth, having the father of the child with them during the labor and birth was a part of a very beautiful experience that they felt the desire to share, and to them it was the sharing that made the experience complete. A large portion of the other women wanted someone with them during the labour, but not during the birth. These women regarded the birth as a difficult painful process that they preferred to do on their own as quickly as possible. One woman said, ''It would only have hurt him (husband) to see me in such pain.''

When I asked if they felt that their attitudes towards pregnancy had changed since they had had the child, all agreed that it had. About half the women had regarded pregnancy and childbirth with a moderate amount of fear and apprehension, having listened to others tell about the pain involved. Some had looked forward to the experience with anticipation while others accepted it as an eventuality, and had given it little thought. Most women felt that their feelings towards pregnancy were quite positive after the birth of their child. Some told of fulfilment, others ecstasy. However, twenty per cent of the women also spoke of depression, of being frightened with the prospect of total responsibility for another human being, of feeling tied down completely with this responsibility.

One woman said: "The six weeks after delivery can have their difficulties. No one expects you to be depressed. Your doctor doesn't see you during this time. This post-natal period needs investigation and education."

My next question dealt with whether they felt that they were sufficiently prepared for the pregnancy, physically, psychologically, emotionally, mentally, intellectually. Two thirds of those women who had planned pregnancies and who intended to have their babies by natural childbirth felt that they were prepared in all respects. They attended classes, saw movies, read a host of literature on the subject, and were in frequent contact with other pregnant women. The other third of this group felt that they were physically prepared for the experience, but that they lacked emotional support, either from those closest to them, or from their doctors. Some women felt that is was not preparation for the pregnancy and birth that was important, but preparation for the adjustment to caring for the child after it was born.

I was surprised by the number of women who relied totally on their doctors for intellectual preparation. Three of the women read no literature, but awaited the monthly visit to their obstetrician for information as to what was happening regarding the progression of the pregnancy, and listened carefully when he briefly told them what would happen during the birth itself. They were instructed to leave everything to his discretion and they felt quite secure in doing this.

I asked the women to sum up the experience of pregnancy and child-birth in terms of positive or negative experience. One woman replied:

A little of both, but mainly positive. The dark sort of mystery about childbirth and about my body was broken; the birth was, of course,

141

hard work, but thoroughly involving and so fully satisfying as a complete experience of body-mind, that for several days after, I was in a very 'unreal' state of fully sensing myself as an animal being, my child as my offspring, my existence as being fully grounded in nature.

Another said:

A lot of both. I felt intensely up and down throughout. Sometimes I cried for joy; sometimes I cried in fear. But it was the most total experience of my life. I'm a better person, more in touch with life, for having been heavy with child and given birth to it.

Section two of my interviews and questionnaire dealt with the family. Exactly half of my subjects were pleased with their husband's response to the pregnancy and birth. They felt that they were involved, helpful and supportive which is what they, the women, had expected and wanted. The other half were not satisfied with their husband's (or boyfriend's) response to the situation. One woman remarked cynically, "Surprised, but tolerant." Another said, "It was my pregnancy. He didn't feel very involved. Sometimes he expressed regret that we wouldn't be able to travel around as easily, and be more tied down to earning money, once we had a child." One unmarried woman, living in a co-operative said:

My parents regretted that I wasn't married, but they were both happy they would have a grandchild and assured me that they would love it as they did their others. They would have liked to share the news, but were ashamed to. The people living in my house were interested in my stories about the baby's progress and what childbirth would be like, etc.

Another unmarried mother said,

My boyfriend was unprepared for the news and it took him a while to adjust to my being pregnant. My mother's main concern was getting her pregnant daughter married. The people living with me were surprised (shocked), but they were happy when they saw that I was glad to be in the family way. I would have been happier if my family could have accepted my pregnancy, and forgotten about the stigma attached to me as an unwed mother. But they kept pushing me to get married. Once I did they became helpful, though more out of duty than out of any real feeling of affection or desire to be supportive.

When I asked those women who were not satisfied with their family's response to their pregnancy what they would have preferred, one woman answered for all when she said:

142

I wish my husband would have been more excited and willing to participate in reading the books with me, doing the exercises, etc. Also, I wish we could have spent more time talking about what it would be like once we had our baby, so we could have been more prepared. But it seemed he didn't want to think about that. I guess I wanted the baby much more than he did. I really went through much of it alone, though I never felt alone when my baby was inside me. The loneliness comes later when they take him from you.

Five of the women didn't feel satisfied with their parents' or inlaws' reaction to their pregnancy, saying that they were too doting, and expected them to curb normal activities, and nagged when this didn't happen. The remainder had somewhat the same reaction from parents and inlaws, but had enjoyed the extra attention and concern.

Two of the women, who taught small children during the pregnancy itself, felt that probably the most wonderful thing about the whole event was sharing it with a group of youngsters who never tired of hearing about the baby's progress and who squealed in delight when they were able to feel the baby move.

Regarding day to day interactions, most women agreed that there had been a change, either during the pregnancy, or since. "Pregnancy and having a child seems to have put me in a more serious category of life — men don't flirt as much, women don't come by just to fool around. I suppose this is quite natural."

It was surprising to note that eighty per cent of the women did not work at all during the pregnancy. Of those who were working, only two stayed on beyond the fifth month of pregnancy. One woman spoke of her struggle to keep her job in spite of the pregnancy. She talked of the pressure exerted both by her supervisor and her co-workers. Co-workers felt that they would have to assume responsibility for tasks that they believed she would not be able to perform because of her pregnancy. Her supervisor did not feel that it was proper for a pregnant woman who was 'showing' to be working in a public place. She spoke rather bitterly of her struggle to keep the job, and how eventually she was ousted at the end of the eighth month of her pregnancy, and of the difficulty of supporting herself during this period. (This was prior to the government's pregnancy leave with pay.)

Three of the women that I interviewed were not married at the time of their pregnancies. Though they felt that friends were eager to be supportive and became far more considerate, they were unhappy with the reaction of casual acquaintances, and those who were working expressed displeasure with their interactions with co-workers. They felt that co-workers could not understand how an unwed mother could be happy with a pregnancy. One woman felt that her co-workers became patronizing and were not above moralizing regarding pregnancies out of wedlock, and the stigma that they felt would be attached to the child. All three resented the unsolicited pity bestowed upon them.

My next questions dealt with the medical aspect of the pregnancy. I was interested to know if most of the women were aware of pertinent information, such as the different types of births it would be possible to have, the different kinds of anaesthetics and their value and consequences. Five of the women did not have possession of this information. Three of the five felt that it was not necessary, that this part of the pregnancy and birth should be left in the hands of the 'expert', i.e. the doctor. The other two expressed regret over not being better informed and felt that the fault was the doctors', who did not think that it was necessary for an expectant mother to know these things. When I inquired as to why they did not ask their doctors about it, they replied that they were intimidated by them and did not feel free to initiate a discussion of this kind. One mentioned that her obstetrician was always in a rush and that she felt that she would be imposing upon his valuable time should she request more information.

I was pleased that so many of the women were indeed in possession of this information. However, when I asked them to elaborate, most of them were unable to do so. I did not expect them to remember clinical jargon, rather general theories regarding cervical blocks, epidurals, different effects of various types of general anaesthesia. The women, with the exception of three, said that they were told by their doctors what kind of anaesthetic would be administered, if it were necessary, but that they were not fully conscious of the value and consequences of the anaesthetic that was administered, nor of other anaesthetics. These women went on to say that they were quite satisfied with their doctor's choice of anaesthetic, but if they were to have another pregnancy, would prefer to discuss the subject more fully, and then have some say in the choice.

One woman had her baby by caesarean section. It should be mentioned that she had intended to have the baby by natural childbirth without anaesthetics of any kind, and was crushed to hear that a caesarean would be necessary, losing all interest in knowing what would be done to her.

The three women who were very knowledgeable about the
144

subject had their babies without anaesthetics of any kind, but felt that possession of the information was important should complications have arisen.

Most of the women were aware to a limited extent of the different types of deliveries. Two of the women only knew about vaginal deliveries and caesarean sections. The remainder, again with the exception of three women, knew generally about the different types of deliveries, i.e. head first, breech birth, transverse presentation, caesarean section. None were fully aware of the implications of the different types of deliveries. Two women expressed the opinion that they preferred not to know, indicating that being knowledgeable about the subject would have made them worry needlessly during the pregnancy itself, and may have caused more fear during the delivery.

Sometimes it may do more harm than good. A high strung nervous woman will perhaps worry needlessly with too much information. Major decisions must be the doctor's; a life is involved and a semi-educated mother may choose the wrong thing.

Another said, "I feel it depends on each person individually. I was the type that had faith in the doctor and therefore did not question the situation." This woman went on to say:

When my child was of school age, I became employed by Child Health Association where I learned and gained a wealth of experience and realized then how fortunate young mothers are in having the opportunity to attend classes regarding pregnancy and childbirth, and how well they are prepared to deal with their babies when care, health, and behaviour problems arose.

The three women who were very knowledgeable regarding different types of deliveries as well as of implications of them felt that it was very important to be in possession of this information. They all expressed the desire to understand what was happening, and all three verbalized the importance of being fully in control of the situation. One said: "A woman must be as well informed as possible, and made to feel that the things that her body and mind are telling her are quite respectable. Out of that, I think, will come control and a good result, instead of a confused or even horrid time."

The women who were partially knowledgeable about types of delivery usually said that, in retrospect, they would have preferred to be more completely in control of the situation. "Yes. After all it is one's body which is undergoing changes and it is vital to be aware of what is happening and why." Another

145

said, "Yes, I do. Once you have lost control all kinds of fears may start to build up." Another said, "Yes, though I can't really explain why. I guess I think one should always be in control of any situation." One woman interestingly stated, "Yes. If I had been in control when my child was born, possibly I would not be frightened to have another one now." Also:

> Yes! But we must be better informed first. The experience belongs to us and those who can share it with us. We must not give up this experience. No one can do it for us. They can only rob us of the fullness of the experience. It is a time of heightened consciousness. We shouldn't let them drug our minds or make us feel we're incapable of making important decisions while we're giving birth. We are such powerful, beautiful creatures when we give birth.

I was curious to know where the women obtained information regarding pregnancy and childbirth. As I have already mentioned, five women were almost totally without medical knowledge, save what they picked up haphazardly from other mothers. In most cases, information amassed this way consisted of gruesome, exaggerated tales, and all five women said that they did not take it seriously, though two said that it did manage to make them a little more apprehensive. One remarked regretfully, "All my doctor told me was that I was pregnant."

Those who had a fair amount of information regarding pregnancy and birth obtained some of it from their obstetrician, some from books, some from valuable discussions with other pregnant women, or mothers. In almost every case, the discussions with the obstetrician were initiated by the women themselves.

Some prepared lists and initiated discussion at each monthly visit. Many bought paperback publications and browsed through them for an insight into the event. Women who were really well prepared and knowledgeable were those women who had taken natural childbirth classes, seen movies, read a great deal of literature, visited hospital maternity wards, labour and delivery rooms, who had spoken with women who had "rooming-in" and were able to weigh the advantages and disadvantages of this practice. These women also spoke favorably about their obstetricians, viewing them more in the role of helper and coach, rather than boss.

I concluded both the interviews and questionnaire with the question: "Do you believe that pregnancy and childbirth are necessarily, or naturally, heavy, often painful experiences?" Nine of the women refused to call it a painful experience, but were definitely of the opinion that there was a great deal of pain involved in the birth process. However, they were cheerful about this 'fact' and rather martyr-like, making such statements as: "True, it is painful, but in a good frame of mind it is certainly bearable." "Unless circumstances are extremely unusual, there is no pain forgotten as soon or as easily as childbirth pain." "The hardest part of the pregnancy brings such exquisite results." I am reminded of a speech given by Pope Pious X, who stated that the more pain felt by a woman in labor, the more the woman would love her child. Another woman said quietly, "For me it was frightening."

Fifteen women, who refused to regard it as a heavy painful process, stated that it was a matter of physical and mental preparation. Those who were prepared physically, whose muscles were toned up and ready to work, and who understood the process, and who did not let fear prevent the body from doing its thing, felt that it could be a very enjoyable, even ecstatic experience.

One of the most striking things about gathering information such as this was the difficulty I had in contacting the women. It served to make me acutely aware of how isolated we are in our segregated nuclear families, living in our closed cubicles, out of touch with each other's experience. Though I promised to draw no profound conclusions on the basis of this study, I can't restrain myself from stating that pregnancy and childbirth seems to me to be another area in which women continue to be fucked over by a repressive, discriminating system, even to the point of accepting fear and pain as something inherent in childbirth. If nothing else, this paper might serve as an impetus for women to get together to talk about these things, find solutions, deal with ego-tripping doctors, post-partum blues, and the difficulty of raising children on our own.

What do pregnant women read about pregnancy and childbirth?

A publication rapidly becoming prominent on the pregnant woman's best seller list is *The New Childbirth*[1] by Erna Wright, S.R.N., S.C.M., an Englishwoman and practising nurse. The book is about something called 'psychoprophylaxis' which literally means 'mind-prevention.' It involves the elimination of old fears and practices, substituting new information and techniques. The book was written for two groups of people. First, expectant parents who have heard about natural childbirth, which the author terms 'the new childbirth', and who are isolated from those who could teach it to them. For them it is a practical guide, complete with information regarding what the expectant mother will experience from the moment childbirth begins. It includes a detailed section on the physical and mental training required for a happy healthy pregnancy and childbirth. Second, Wright hopes that midwives, health-visitors, and physiotherapists dealing with expectant mothers will use this as a handbook, or reference material in their work. "My dearest wish would be fulfilled if midwives worked together with their patients, following the training through, and thus were partners in this exciting adventure — active parenthood."

The book was first inspired by the teachings of Dr. Grantly Dick Read whose published works deal primarily with the philosophy behind childbirth free of pain and fear, rather than a "how-to" approach. Later, Erna Wright worked with Dr. Pierre Vellay, a follower of Dr. Fernand Lamaze, and learned the practical side of childbirth free of pain.

On the whole, she provides a straightforward, easy to understand and follow handbook. Her style is a simplistic one, often slightly patronizing in tone. The book is well illustrated with drawings by Gilliam Bayens, diagrams by Christopher Mason, and some very lovely photographs by John Minshall of a woman giving birth with a huge smile on her face, reaching for the child as it makes its entrance into the world.

Wright could have confined herself to the field she is obviously expert in: the practicalities of natural childbirth. Unfortunately she ventures beyond this and attempts a little prosyletizing. She discusses the behaviour to expect from the as yet unborn female child:

> Here's one thing for instance, that a little girl will do. Say you decide to put her into panties instead of nappies for the first time ... So you put her into panties and you don't say anything, just to see how it goes. You'll find that within the hour she'll find some man — it could be her father or an uncle, the milkman or the postman, the first man to come along. And she'll say to him "Look, panties!"
>
> You'll be terribly embarrassed. How can *your* daughter behave like this? But your daughter does behave like this because biologically she is already doing a very feminine thing in drawing attention to her body. And it's her instinct to draw this attention unerringly from a man and not from a woman:[2]

Considering that the book was printed in New York in 1969, this attitude is quite a mind-blower.

Another book that several women mentioned reading is *Husbands and Pregnancy* by William H. Genné.[3] This book attempts to involve the father through leading him to understand what is happening to his wife during the pregnancy and childbirth.

It, too, is written in a simplistic, at times patronizing, style.

In order to start from a frame of reference that a man might understand, Genné makes several interesting comparisons of the wife to the automobile.

> In the rush and busyness of life, we accumulate negative feelings just as a car motor accumulates carbon. Like carbon these feelings cut down our efficiency. To get a good "mechanic" to help us understand our feelings is no sign of failure or disgrace, anymore than getting our car overhauled is a sign of failure or neglect.[4]

Another comparison of this genre is made when Genné tries to explain morning sickness: "We can understand why it happens if we remember that our wives are 'shifting gears' inside."[5] In an effort to encourage men to encourage their wives to do more exercises, he states rather truthfully: "Many of our wives were typists or had other sedentary jobs. Many of them are in rather poor shape when we consider their muscles, particularily those of the pelvic area."[6] He also explains[7] that during labour, a medic will periodically examine the wife's progress, rectally, in order to avoid infection.

According to Dr. Kinch, head of ob./gyn. at the Montreal General, this is inaccurate information. A rectal examination is far more painful for a woman than a vaginal examination, and there is no scientific evidence that there are fewer instances of infection from it.

With shady ulterior motives, Genné suggests to husbands that they encourage their wives to breastfeed the baby;

> Breast feeding is also good from the point of view of the husband. The new baby is usually fed around two o'clock in the morning. If the baby is bottle fed, your wife will expect you to take your turn at this ungodly hour. If the baby is breast fed, you can hand it to her and go back to sleep.[8]

Medical doctors who presume themselves to be specialists in human behaviour as well, are annoying. Genné is guilty of the same presumptuousness as Wright is in this respect:

> Your son will come to learn how a masculine man feels, thinks and acts. How does a real man talk and dress? What kinds of work does a real man do? How does a real man act with other men? How does he act with women? How does a real man show his emotions?[9]

Regarding the unborn female child, he says, "If you have a daughter, you will want her to grow up and be happily married."[10]

Pregnancy and Birth by Alan F. Guttmacher, M.D.[11] was the book third on the list of most frequently read books by expectant parents. It is a straightforward manual, thoroughly covering most aspects of childbearing. It is written in a clear, factual manner and is not encumbered with so much technical jargon that a lay reader can't decipher the message. At the same time the reader is not treated as an unintelliigent being, for Guttmacher does provide her with pertinent medical information and terminology.

He is careful to outline the theory behind the practice, which is another strong point in his favour. This leaves the reader the leeway of choosing the technique, anaesthetic, etc. that makes most sense to her.

The only criticism that I have for this book, is that it does not go far enough in encouraging women to have children by natural childbirth, which may be an unfair value judgement on my part.

The Canadian Mother & Child, a publication by the Department of National Health and Welfare, Third Edition, fourth printing, 1970, is superficial in that it does not explore the different theories behind pregnancy and specifically childbirth. The message throughout the book is "trust your doctor, he knows best," a message that women, as I have shown above, find repressive and frustrating; a message that does not always hold true. This book's cursory treatment of the stages of pregnancy does not provide the complete, in-depth information most expectant parents desire, and compared to Guttmacher's book, it is second rate, hardly worth consulting.

Husband-Coached Childbirth by Robert A. Bradley, M.D.,[12] is a fine piece of work by a doctor who sees his role as that of coach and helper. He has presided at more than 7000 unmedicated births, working with expectant parents who had been taught how to make pregnancy and childbirth a joyous, painless experience. "Generally, mothers prefer to walk back with the father from the delivery room holding the baby, and in many cases mother and baby go home with father two hours after the birth is finished." His style is simple, sincere, without undertones of chauvinism. He discusses pregnancy and childbirth from a humanistic perspective, always keeping the feelings of the prospective parents uppermost in importance. I would venture to say that this book is a must for parents planning to have their child by natural childbirth, together. Certainly it puts pregnancy into a very healthy perspective.

Grantly Dick Read's *Childbirth Without Fear*[13] has become
150

a classic in the field of pregnancy. First published under the title *Natural Childbirth*, in 1933 in England, it presents a possible theory of natural childbirth, and its application during pregnancy and parturition. ''This task has not been undertaken for academic reasons, but rather as a further step towards proof of the philosophic principle that all progress, both moral and physical, ultimately depends upon the perfection of motherhood.'' Read discusses fear of and during childbirth as a conditioned reflex and explores the agents which condition women to accept fear and pain in childbirth as natural. He also has a chapter in which he discusses the ignorance of women regarding pregnancy and childbirth, as a fear-producing, pain-causing factor in the birth process. His contentions are supported by endless anecdotes of his experience, making an interesting, thought-provoking bit of reading. It is debatable as to whether he should be criticised for being a little too sentimental about the birth of a child.

The Womanly Art of Breastfeeding, a publication by the La Leche League[14] is frequently mentioned as good reading material for expectant mothers. Though it does not provide any information regarding the pregnancy and birth, other than to indicate how these processes affect breastfeeding, it does break many of the myths that both men and women have about women's breasts and the ability of women to breastfeed. In North America pervasive breast fetishism has caused the breast to become so far removed from its biological function, that most women presume that breast-feeding is something too difficult to attempt. This book destroys this myth, and attempts to restore women's confidence in their bodies as something other than object. It does however, have a stereotyped attitude to women's roles within the family.

Pour Vous Future Maman by Trude Sekely is a Montreal publication,[15] containing well organized exercises for the pregnant woman; exercises that tone up the body in general and muscles to be used during childbirth, including breathing techniques, in particular. It is a fine handbook to be used in conjunction with natural childbirth classes. The last chapter contains testimonials by parents who worked with Sekely during their pregnancies. They all describe the marvels of natural childbirth. A long playing record has also been prepared by her. Side one deals with tone up exercises and side two takes the listener through the birth process, stage by stage, with methods of breathing and positions to assume for a comfortable, joyous, painless experience.

Last but not least, *Having a Right-On Baby*, by Faith H. Liebert,[16] an eighteen page pamphlet urging women to stand

151

up for their right to have their children their way, to stop being intimidated by ego-tripping doctors, to become better informed about the pregnancy and childbirth process, is a well intentioned pamphlet by a radical woman. Though she treats the process in a very cursory way, she does list publications to consult should the reader decide to have a "right-on baby." One of the books she mentions is *Thank-you, Dr. Lamaze*, by Marjory Karmel. I did read this book a couple of years ago and remember it as a good account of a woman's natural childbirth experience with Dr. Lamaze in Paris, and then of her search for an obstetrician in the U.S., during her second pregnancy, someone who would treat her pregnancy as a meaningful dignified process, without anaesthetics and without fear or pain.

There are many more publications on the subject, and unfortunately too few good ones. A partial list of these publications is included with this paper. I would suggest that nine months' time is ample to consult most of the publications, and I would urge expectant parents to do so, in the belief that knowledgeable thinking parents are happier parents.

Notes

1. Universal Publishing and Distributing Corp., New York, 1969.
2. *Ibid.*, p. 62.
3. Association Press, 1956.
4. *Ibid.*, p. 14.
5. *Ibid.*, p. 30.
6. *Ibid.*, p. 41.
7. *Ibid.*, p. 67.
8. *Ibid.*, p. 86.
9. *Ibid.*, p. 106.
10. *Ibid.*, p. 107.
11. New American Library, New York, 1962.
12. Harper & Row, New York, 1965.
13. Harper & Brothers, New York, 1944.
14. Franklin Park, Illinois, 1963.
15. Editions de l'Homme, 1965.
16. Radical Education Project, Detroit.

Partial List of Publications on Pregnancy & Childbirth

Better Homes & Gardens, *Better Homes & Gardens Baby Book,* Bantam Books, New York, N.Y., 1970, 383 pp.

Bing, Elisabeth, *Six Practical Lessons for an Easier Childbirth,* Bantam Books, New York, N.Y., 1969, 128 pp.

Birch, William G., M.D., *a doctor discusses pregnancy,* Budlong Press Co., Chicago, Ill., 1969. 114 pp.

Bradley, Robert A., M.D., *Husband-Coached Childbirth,* Harper & Row, Publishers, Inc., New York, N.Y., 1965, 208 pp.

Carnation Company, Ltd., *You and Your Contented Baby,* Canada, 1966, 32 pp.

Davis, Adelle, *Let's Have Healthy Children,* Harcourt, Brace & World, Inc., New York, 1959, 314 pp.

Department of National Health and Welfare, Child and Maternal Health Division, *The Canadian Mother and Child,* Queen's Printer for Canada, Ottawa, 1970. 173 pp.

Department of National Health and Welfare, Child and Maternal Health Division, *Posture and Rest Positions for Expectant Mothers,* The Queen's Printer, Ottawa, 1969. 11 pp.

Genné, William H., *Husbands and Pregnancy,* Association Press, New York, N.Y., 1956, 127 pp.

Guttmacher, M.D., Alan F., *Pregnancy and Birth,* The New American Library, Inc., for the Viking Press, New York, 1962, 286 pp.

Israel M.D., S. Leon & Rubin, M.D., Isadore, *Sexual Relations During Pregnancy and the Post-Delivery Period,* Sex Information and Education Council of the U.S., 1967, 21 pp.

Karmel, Marjory, *Thank-you, Dr. Lamaze* (Publisher unknown)

La Leche League International, *The Womanly Art of Breastfeeding,* Franklin Park, Illinois, 1963. 166 pp.

Liebert, Faith H., *Having a Right-on Baby,* Radical Education Project, Detroit, Michigan, 18 pp.

Maternity Center Association, *Preparation for Childbearing,* Maternity Center Association, New York, N.Y., 1970. 45 pp.

Read, Grantly Dick, *Childbirth Without Fear,* Harper & Brothers Publishers, New York, 1944. 257 pp.

Rodale, J. I., *Natural Health and Pregnancy,* Pyramid Publications, Inc., New York, N.Y., 1968. 320 pp.

Sekely, Trude, *Pour vous Future Maman,* Les Editions de l'Homme, Montréal, 1965, 175 pp.

Spock, Dr. Benjamin, *Baby and Child Care,* Simon & Schuster of Canada, Ltd., Richmond Hill, Ontario, 1971. 620 pp.

Warner, M.D., Marie Pichel, *a doctor discusses breast feeding,* Budlong Press Co., Chicago, Illinois, 1970. 102 pp.

Wright, Erna, *The New Childbirth,* Universal Publishing and Distributing Corporation, 1969, New York, N.Y. 244 pp.

ABORTION IN QUEBEC

by

Janet Kask

If you want an abortion in Quebec, a woman was heard to comment, you'd better start making arrangements for it two weeks before you conceive. It sounds strange, but the fact is that legal abortions in Quebec are perilously scarce for the woman without good medical connections at the "right" hospital.

Only a handful of Montreal hospitals perform abortions and they service the entire province. Whether or not a hospital board allows abortions to be performed depends on how staff doctors interpret 1969 changes in the Criminal Code making hospital abortions legal when a woman's physical and mental health is "seriously endangered." The vast majority of Quebec hospitals and social agencies are influenced by Roman Catholic doctrine which considers abortion immoral.

This situation puts a serious strain on four Montreal hospitals — the Montreal General, Jewish General, Catherine Booth and Reddy Memorial — which perform most of the legal abortions in Quebec. Their facilities are usually booked up at least two months in advance, creating the critical situation that prompted the remark about making plans "two weeks before you conceive."

Of the 20,000 Quebec women who had abortions in 1971 (a Montreal doctor's educated guess) less than 1,000 had them performed legally in Quebec hospitals under Medicare. Most of them may have had a doctor working in one of the previously mentioned hospitals that interpret health as a social and emotional as well as a physical state.

The rest of the women didn't have the time or the courage for the labyrinth of hospital red tape. Some went to Ontario until hospitals, in Ottawa at least, started closing their doors to outsiders

154

because of overcrowding.

Those with enough money went to New York State where abortion requires only an agreement between the woman and her doctor, but costs from $185 to $1,000. Or they went underground, if they were lucky enough to find the right referral system, and had a safe, illegal abortion by one of four or five qualified Montreal doctors. The cost generally ranges from $150 to $300. One "underground" agency averages 50 private referrals a week.

Many women, lacking money for a proper operation, sought other means. Some tried aborting themselves or had friends or husbands try to do it. Others went to "quack" abortionists. Hundreds suffered serious complications. Dozens died.

A recent San Francisco study reports that illegal abortion was the most common cause of maternal death before women had access to legal hospital abortions. An estimated 100 in every 100,000 cases died. In Hungary where abortion has been legal for years, the death rate between 1964 and 1967 was 1.2 per 100,000.

The crisis will go on until more doctors and hospital administrations change their views on abortion. Women will continue to pay high fees for a service they're already paying for through taxes. Unrestricted illegal abortionists will continue to live high off the misery — and some, the tragedy — of women. Consider the tax-free income from five to 10 abortions daily at $300 each.

A small group of dedicated women will continue to carry the counselling load.

"If every Quebec hospital did its share, there wouldn't be a problem," says Dr. Peter Gillett of the Montreal General Hospital.

"The hospital beds for pregnancies are there. An estimated one in four pregnancies is unwanted. The bed is needed either way. A hospital could handle as many as five terminations for every maternity case.

Refusing to abort women won't solve the problem. They likely will find other ways out.

"If women don't have unrestricted access to abortion, it's naive to think they're necessarily going to learn to accept and love their unwanted pregnancies," says Dr. Gillett. "They're going to go to an illegal abortionist or they're going to carry the unwanted and unplanned pregnancy to term.

"There's a growing amount of evidence indicating that the latter course is detrimental to the mental health of the mother and the child. The battered child and the child with emotional

155

disturbances later in life is too often the result of an unplanned pregnancy.''

Until birth control methods are safe, foolproof and widely publicized, women will have unwanted pregnancies. If they want to terminate them, they'll find a way.

A nucleus of dedicated volunteers in Montreal is helping hundreds, perhaps thousands of women end unwanted pregnancies. The Family Planning Association recently opened a bilingual birth control information centre that provides, among other advice, abortion counselling. Doctors, social agencies, citizen and youth clinics do their best with limited facilities.

Commercial agencies handling New York referrals have been declared illegal there, but still operate in Quebec. Referral agencies advertising in local newspapers and on FM radio stations work through clinics in New York city and charge a ''deposit'' from a third to a half the price of the abortion which ranges from $185 to $425.

One woman said she works with two clinics, one charging $195 and the other, $235. The latter, she said, gives better service so she encourages her clients to go there. None of these agencies would say how they were financed.

Clinics are situated in New York City rather than closer to the Quebec border because abortions in upstate New York are prohibitively expensive. One agent quoted $575 as the going rate for ''border'' abortions. I was also told by one doctor that some of these organizations were giving out fraudulent information in order to send customers to their clinics. For example, one woman was told it was impossible to get a legal abortion in Montreal.

Women's liberation groups have shouldered most of the burden. At the end of a long line of buck-passing and word-of-mouth referrals, they often have to cope with desperate cases refused by the hospitals. Often these groups have helped raise money for abortion as well as doing counselling.

''The services have been completely overloaded,'' says Marilyn Rowell of the Montreal Coalition for Repeal of the Abortion Law.

''We've had girls arriving from places like Rouyn-Noranda on our doorstep with suitcases in hand, crying. They'd been told by their local doctors to show up at the Montreal General or Jewish General hospitals where they'd be looked after.

''Of course the hospitals couldn't take them, so they sent them to us. And they're usually without much money.''

156

The situation deteriorated last fall when a political split at the Women's Centre on Ste. Famille St., where counselling was done by French and English-speaking women's liberation groups, resulted in a French-only policy. A woman from the Front de Libération de la Femme which runs the relocated service downtown, assured me that any woman will get counselling if she speaks French or brings along a translator.

A group of McGill women from the coalition subsequently opened a bilingual birth control and abortion counselling office. They didn't really want to duplicate services already available, one of their group said, but the demand for a co-ordinated English-language agency was getting out of hand.

Abortion counselling is a heavy business. The subject has been underground for so long that few people are equipped to deal with it. The women involved are the first to admit this.

"It was an incredible responsibility," said one student. "It consumed every minute I had. I was getting phone calls at home around the clock.

"Counsellors need to know more about what to expect during and after abortions. Experiences vary with the woman. I felt I didn't know enough."

Is this an ideal situation?

As one doctor remarked: "It's not the repeal of the abortion law that counts, but the repeal of doctors' attitudes. If doctors would recognize the need for unrestricted access to hospital abortions performed by qualified personnel, such abortions could easily be done within the context of the present law."

A SINGLE PARENT TURNS OFF AND ON

Some sunny morning
with sky all bright and clear
I'll pack a bag and go away
and never come back here
sweet children
do not want a friend
in mother and I cry!
an end an end!
an end to all this loving dear ...
Respect restraint and debt that weights
that weighs because tradition says!
get out get out all mothers
get out from under foot
and let the dear departed
have rest from childer's boot.
There is no cause or reason
to stay since he is gone
and all my life is worthless
quite fit to throw away
disposable is what we are
the new synthetic breed
a parent so disposable
he hardly is a need.
So up with test-tube babies
and harvest just prime seed
away away with womanhood

male sperm is all we need
and when we have dispensed with love
and passion and emotion
we'll all go back past embryos
to blobs of mental motion
aided and exceed by
the robot and computer
which well develop out
to be more useful and much cuter.
Disposable the human race
will go away without a trace.
The robot and computer will rust away abused
and earth can then disintegrate
because it is unused
if we all pack our little bag
and give up parenthood.

Mary Yuill

LETTER TO ABSENT CHILD:

In you
I invested my loneness
and received your loneness;
invested my yearning
and reaped strange yearning;
invested my doubts
and grew other doubts.

What makes any one think
that loneness invested
multiplies into companionship
or yearning into fulfilment
or doubts into certainty?

But I miss the response
that was more than an echo
and less than a confirmation.

inge packer

This poem was first published in *Viewpoints,* V, 4, 1970/71.

NEGOTIATION

My artist sits and doodles on her napkin in the restaurant.
I watch and see a head of a clown appear
In many-pointed cap and bells.
A friendly clown, but sharp, definitive,
With certain nose and mouth determined, strong.
The bells are blossoms in full bloom.
     I, smiling, ask,
"Who is it, you or I, my Sweet?"
And soon, a wall appears
With nick behind the clown-head,
And another head, with child-clown's eyes and nose,
Eager and uncertain,
With single-pointed cap and button,
and no bloom,
Peers down through nick above the wall.
     A branch of tree appears.
Oh no! The child-clown's hand,
Kerchief in it, cheering Big Clown on.
And still beyond it, up,
From small clown's other unseen hand,
A string, — high, higher reaching,
Tangling on the way to kite, —
A many-layered interlocking structure, —
Daring, light, and rising in the wind!
     We speak of many other things, my child and I,
     And smile into each other's eyes and know,
     And quietly, as we both rise to go,
     I lift my eyes in gratitude
     And put the napkin in my bag.

by Shulamith S. Yelin

THE QUESTION OF SEXUALITY

Sexuality is something that women are trying to discuss among themselves while finding such discussions extremely difficult. My class tried to debate this issue several times, but, each time, we would end up talking about motherhood. Women in consciousness-raising groups sometimes need more than two years of regular meetings, before sexuality can become an openly discussed matter. ''Too long has the whole process of love-making and marriage been wrapped up in mystery,'' said Nellie McClung in 1916.

If this chapter on the Question of Sexuality contains a few poems only, it is precisely for that reason.

M.A.

The influence of the moon on WOMEN'S MINDS

After a 17th Century Engraving

Freda Bain /71

FOUR POEMS

out of mercy
come clean away
my lust or
i shall swallow my fingers,
a hungry schoolgirl.

a slave of Love,
i obey
the Man,
contented, like a cut flower.

and afterwards,
without a single sound,
he left the room to play hockey.

i met a perfect man
who could last with a woman of my kind,
months,
and then go away completely
having devoured
everything i owned inside.

mary melfi

165

I fear
    the vast space
        we have between us
          when we touch
I fear the yawning chasm of your approach
I fear
    the winds that rise and howl
    when we whisper
    in each other's ear
I fear
    the hollow-bellied fires
    that spark our starved union
I fear
    that you will never grow eyes
    to see the eternal signs
    through which the touch comes

Margit Boronkay

TOUCHED-UNTOUCHED

You have come
      rage Rage RAGE
I lie here, you sleep, your world so narrow
      I am alone, so alone
You touched me, I, untouched,
      Unaware - how, so unaware? How, so unconscious?
      Man of the World
The world is here now
      but gone, the moment for me.
I lie alone; you know me not
      your seed within me
      I untouched touched untouched

Beatrice Pearson

OCTOBER

If you touched me
put your hand beneath my head
came up behind me
and said my name
and turning, I looked into your eyes
I would be one with you again.
Out of self and part of together
like the pages of a book
between soft leather-covers
like the trees around the house
the sun around the day
the moon that rings the night
out of nowhere into somewhere
would that be for me.

Mary Yuill

RAINY DAY

The windowpane
with wobbly tracks
of raindrops
running down their backs
the attic roof
my music-box
with rhythmic
syncopating knocks
tell everyone
to go away
I need to be
alone to-day.

Mary Yuill

WOMEN'S LIBERATION

For generations women have been thinking, and thought without expression is dynamic and gathers volume by repression. EVOLUTION WHEN BLOCKED AND SUPPRESSED BECOMES REVOLUTION.

Nellie McClung, 1916

MAN'S NIGHTMARE OR WOMAN'S FANTASY
by
Sharron Lee Smith

The human male will be necessary in the future, but his role is going to differ radically from that which he now performs. The majority of the males are going to be eunuchs, while the limited number of surviving and potent males will contribute to sperm banks.

Male children will be raised on health farms knowing neither their mother nor their forecast. The ones selected to be eunuchs will be castrated before the age of puberty, removed from the farms and placed in a working atmosphere. The education of the male will be controlled to prevent advanced intellectual development resulting in a bid for equality with the female. The males will be simply workers, servants to those superior human beings known as females.

Eunuchs will do all the heavy manual labour such as construction of buildings, bridges and highways; they will be the sanitary engineers, undertakers, window-washers, performing all other tasks requiring the superior muscular attributes of the male. Eunuchs will be totally masculine except for their inability to procreate. To control the sexual drive, the eunuchs will be fed saltpetre.

After those few males who have not been castrated have made adequate contribution to the sperm banks they too will be emasculated, or, if they so desire, exterminated. The reproduction of the population will be restrained.

Because women have an extra sense known as feminine intuition, they will make excellent political leaders and administrators in the armed forces. They will be able to run schools, businesses and hospitals much more efficiently by applying and combining both their compassion and circumspection. Since ignorance is bliss, the need for sexual satisfaction will be a foreign feeling to most women. Should the need arise, however, devices such as dildoes may be used. Lesbianism and masturbation will no longer be frowned upon or forbidden. Divorce, widowhood, whoredom, adultery and incest will be unknown.

The pattern of living will be much as it is today except that females will monopolize the world as the rulers and leaders. No longer will women be terrified to be out alone after dark nor will they be placed in a compromising situations by overly aggressive males. Men as they are known today simply will not exist and the world will be pink.

CONSCIOUSNESS-RAISING

by

Anuradha Bose

Consciousness-raising is an integral part of the Women's Liberation Movement. It is the first definite sign that all is not well with hearth and home, that the move towards women's politicization as women has begun.

Consciousness-raising is commonly confused with group therapy and lumped together with T-groups, encounter groups and sensitivity training. Actually, it is radically different from all these. Consciousness-raising deals with feelings, sentiments, emotions, gut reactions — the few attributes allowed us as women. It uses, maybe even exploits, these through intimate talk-sessions free of the element of role-playing and without 'objective guidance' (usually of a man!) For consciousness-raising groups have no discussion leaders. It refutes the traditional leader-led roles, the dominant-passive syndromes and the need for a hierarchy.

Consciousness-raising is a subjective thing. Each woman talks specifically about herself and her experiences. Generalising, rationalising and theorising is scrupulously avoided. The rest of the group listen to her, examine her experiences and then give

174

testimony themselves. It is a supportive talk-session and an 'emotion-storming,' where women discover their new identities, where they discuss their frustrations and fears, give vent to their anger, without fear of reprobation and ridicule. The primary function of the group is to enable each woman to explore herself, her relationship to men, her relationships with other women and also to a society where she finds herself in an oppressed interest group.

Consciousness-raising, as a formal tool, is new, but the process is as old as Eve. It is the natural extension of the 'Kaffee-Klatsch' but has more purpose to it than a mere 'bitch-session.' It is a commitment women make, to come together and take stock of their personal situations. Women have always complained to each other about picking up after husband and offspring, dirty dishes and diapers — in short about their twenty-four-hour-a-day seven-days-a-week jobs. They had so far seen themselves as isolated instances of 'incipient neuroses,' their gripes as unique to themselves. Suddenly, it struck women that all women were voicing the same complaints and the movement was on.

Consciousness-raising groups usually meet once a week in each other's homes. The ideal number is between three and seven, no larger. This gives every woman her turn in giving testimony and answering questions. Apart from not having a leader, there should be no attempt to structure or formalise these sessions. Discussions must be spontaneous and free-flowing. Any woman can start by merely relating an anecdote or sharing some part of her experience with others. The topics are usually the same and keep recurring. Sex roles, media images, work and housework, personal relationships with men and women are only some of the myriad subjects discussed. In short, the realisation soon dawns that your being a woman is a total study in oppression and that your oppression is total.

The best way to begin is in the beginning, that is from childhood and parent-child relationships and progress through grade-school, the teenage years to marriage and old age. After testimony has been given by every woman, the testimony is closely examined to find common elements in the experiences and extend that commonality to all women.

Consciousness-raising is a very unsettling experience. It reinforces and magnifies a woman's deepest insecurities and breaks down all the elaborate defences behind which women have taken refuge over the years. It sensitizes a woman to her condition and the condition of all women. It eliminates none of a woman's anxieties but creates new tensions. It answers no questions while raising several more.

Once all women within the group become fully aware of their oppression the need for a weekly meeting ceases to exist. There is no real limit on how long a group should last, but they usually last from three months to a year. The sentiments that the women have come to share and the insights that they have gained are often translated into action, either personal or collective. The former is usually the harder transition to make since it may mean deeply painful experiences. Yet, the newfound solidarity within and without the group supports the women through these difficult times. Collective action can take different forms. Involvement in a communal situation, in law reform, abortion repeal are several ways women have taken up cudgels on their own behalf.

I was actively involved in a consciousness-raising group between November 1970 and June 1971. We were seven women, ranging between the ages of eighteen and twenty-seven. Four were students and three were teachers. There were two married women, a divorced woman and one was pregnant. Three lived at home, two, including myself, were heavily involved with men (and good red-blooded chauvinists at that). One woman was black. We represented a good cross-section of English Canadian women.

We met once a week, usually in one woman's downtown apartment for three to four hours. Attendance was very regular, in spite of the inclement Montreal winter. I know that I never missed a meeting.

It was my first intimate contact with women in twenty-seven years. Before this, I had known women as colleagues, rivals, wives-of-husband's-friends, co-workers and cleaning women. I had had the occasional drink with a girlfriend on a Thursday night or gone out for an afternoon's lunch and shopping. I never had had a real woman friend. I had always got along better with men.

The first time I ever heard of 'Consciousness-Raising' was early in 1970. Susan Brownmiller had published a survey article on the Women's Liberation Movement in the USA in the Sunday magazine Section of the *New York Times*. I called the Women's Centre (now defunct) on Ste-Famille Street and they sent me to a group that was already functioning. I didn't quite fit into the group since it had evolved too far for me to make the necessary adjustment. I called the Women's Centre again and they put me in contact with another group. The woman I called was a bit hesitant when I expressed an interest in joining their group but told me that she would consult the other members. Within a week I heard from her and was invited to join.

I came into the group with plenty of reservations but I shed them along the way. For the first time, I found myself communicating, talking, getting feedback continuously from other women. There was a constant examination of myself and of my experiences — both past and present. Why did I act and react the way I did? How did I feel oppressed? Who was my oppressor? And why did I feel oppressed? I realised how much of a conditioned animal I was and I wasn't ashamed to admit it.

Previously, I had had therapy which had left me feeling 'high' and 'adjusted' only to realise that I had been tutored — or should I say that I had tutored myself into adjusting to somebody else's conception of reality.

I realised now that the anger which I had harboured for years and directed towards certain people and certain institutions and which had made me act unreasonably most of the time, was the anger that most women manifest. It was the anger of an enslaved minority in the face of the oppressor.

I acquired a new feeling of self-worth. It made me surer of myself. I no longer blamed my past inert self on personal faults and unique circumstances. I had discovered women and, incidentally, myself too.

I had learnt to make my situation of an independant, monogamous female live with me. But I realised how much farther I still had to go. I spent the next year, after the group dissolved, reading on the subject of Women's Liberation, doing a lot of self-searching and talking with women. Consciousness-raising is an ongoing process. It takes forms other than a weekly 'rap session.' I continued trying to formulate my position as a woman in a male-oriented society and often felt lost in the labyrinth of my own thoughts. I couldn't quite understand the uncontrollable rages that I flew into when I read a book or watched a film that treated women in a chauvinistic fashion (and their number was legion!) My tolerance level was at a very low ebb and I couldn't respect other people's ideas if they wore different to my own.

Another thing that worried me was that I had lost my capacity to relate to men. I felt that they were all rapacious and I guarded my newly liberated self against them. It was not before I felt completely sure of this new self, that I could start relating to men again. This time on a new basis which seems to warrant much happier results.

NOTES IN MY DIARY

by

Beatrice Pearson

I am 34 years old; have been married for 12 years; the mother of three children (11, 10, 8), I am a full time student at Loyola, wanting to survive it all. So I yield ... I yield to menstruation — I yield to pregnancy — I yield to motherhood — I yield, I yield, I yield, but ...

Where am I? Who am I? I am beautiful and I do survive.

I am here — now yielding only to keep the balance — to keep in tune with my destiny: womanhood, motherhood, wifehood but also humanhood!

Yes, *I am me* and being me, a human, is also part of my destiny. I will not choose between two destinies for both are mine, and no one will force a choice on me. The choice is mine.

DIARY OF A FEMINIST

by

Cerise Morris

I can't pinpoint a moment or an event that precipitated my becoming a feminist; rather there was a growing awareness, accompanied by hurt and outrage, that femininity had connotations of shame, weakness, and inferiority. I grappled with this perceived blow

178

to my self-esteem by exploring "the Woman Question" with a vengeance. In my late teens and early twenties, I voraciously devoured literature on the subject, of which Simone de Beauvoir's writing was the foundation. In so doing, I developed a reasonably coherent understanding of the biological, cultural and ideological forces which shaped and circumscribed the history of women. While this analysis explained things in an adequate and ego-salvaging way, it didn't help me to accept the status quo.

At once the best and worst aspect of my early feminism was the privateness of it. If I had naively assumed that my evolving views would be met with cheers, or at least recognition, I was soon disabused of this notion. Opposition from males was at least predictable, and often took the form of bantering rather than full-scale hostility. Women were another matter. Their smugness, denial, and looks of pity for my 'folly' never ceased to astound me. I was childishly happy whenever I found a woman who had even thought critically about her social definition and role, let alone rejected any part of it. Nevertheless, I admit there was some satisfaction in being a 'rebel', in adopting an unconventional and unpopular stance. With a sharpening sense of irony, I observed the undercurrent of amusement and flirtation running through my 'serious' conversations with men. Because I was young and attractive, my seriousness was cute, my feminism a sexual challenge! Had I been old or unattractive, most of these men would not even have bothered to listen to what I had to say, or would have found it much easier to dismiss me as a 'frustrated broad.'

And so, I fought my little battle on personal fronts; going to university and developing a career plan, rejecting the housewife role, attempting to practice an equalitarian form of marriage, and reacting to specific situations as they arose. All of this was accompanied by doubt, conflict, and some painful choices. Were questions of principle really so important? Wouldn't I be happier if I lost sight of possibly unrealizable goals, and simply adjusted? Was the objective lot of North American women really so bad, after all? Since the majority of women did not express discontentment with their role, was I neurotic in my pre-occupation with female equality?

But I could not alter my basic pattern of self-determination, and I certainly could not shut out my awareness of fundamental injustices suffered by women. I often wished that I could 'do something' about the problem, beyond my personal stance. I imagined a civil rights movement for women, yet knew that when

179

I verbalized this idea I would probably be thought ridiculous, neurotic, or worse. I eagerly pounced on any article, book or public statement by a woman with a feminist orientation, as proof that I was not alone — that others out there were feeling what I felt. When Betty Friedan wrote *The Feminine Mystique,* I felt a sense of triumph; my personal stance was generalized and validated; surely this proved that I hadn't been neurotic all along.

In the past few years my fervor cooled somewhat; not that my convictions had altered, for, in fact, they had solidified. However, one gets deadly bored by innumerable discussions and arguments that never get anywhere, since the same tired terrain is always covered. How many times can you earnestly explain that you do not wish to 'castrate' men, or become an imitation man, or reverse the sexual caste system, or any other perversion of which you are accused; that you *only* claim the right of stretching to your human potential — the potential which has been traditionally denied because of your sex and if this will necessarily affect every social institution, well, sorry about that!

How many times can you deal with the circular reasoning which argues that 'real women' can and do derive their fulfilment through the biological role which Nature has ordained, and society in its wisdom has maintained for them? Eventually, I realized that I was putting myself in the absurd position of attempting to prove that I was human.

I also found that more of my psychic energy was being absorbed by my personal concerns, and less was available for abstract issues, such as The Woman Question. Anyway, I often told myself, as long as women remain unwilling to forego the consolation prizes of their subordinate status (being supported, not having to take full responsibility for their lives, receiving token courtesies, etc.), in pursuit of the abstraction of equality, then nothing is going to change. It seemed that I would have to maintain some uneasy balance between my feminist convictions and the social reality; one which would permit me basic integrity, yet not place me beyond the pale.

Then, along came Women's Lib, with its promise of reopening the can of worms and provoking fresh examination of the basic assumptions about women. As the voice of Women's Lib became louder, more strident, and crossed the border into Canada, all my old feelings resurfaced. I began attending meetings, and was amazed at first by the political awareness of the members, and by their revolutionary fervor. I felt terribly naive and 'Tomish' in comparison to these solemn, radical girls, whose faces were unadulterated by makeup, and who dressed as if for guerilla combat. So I kept my mouth shut, listening and observing. It was so gratifying to hear girls who understood and rejected the whole bill of goods about femininity, and who were organizing to attack some of the structures which oppressed them. At the same time, I noted that the membership was largely young, middle-class, and collegiate. Many of the girls seemed like all-purpose radicals, and I wondered to what extent Women's Liberation was an intellectual game or fad; a luxury afforded them by their youth, class, and student roles. I was also bothered by their adoption of Marxist analysis as practically the official doctrine of the movement. Women's Liberation is seen as being bound up with the liberation of all oppressed groups, and realizable only when a whole socialist revolution takes place.

I take exception to this approach, not so much because I am not a Marxist (for I may yet become one), but because I'm unconvinced that revolution is just over the horizon. I don't feel that the realization of women's demands should depend upon an apocalyptic event, and I am also aware that in societies of every shade on the political spectrum, women are unequal. The analysis of capitalistic class oppression does not seem fully adequate as an explanation of prejudice and discrimination against women.

As I listened to movement women debate the new order of things to come after the revolution, it sometimes seemed that their ideas had little link with reality. I suppose that my orientation is reformist, because just in case the revolution doesn't occur in my lifetime, I would like to see some immediate changes effected within the structures of our present system.

After a few meetings, and exposures to Women's Lib manifestoes, pamphlets, etc., I got the feeling that this radical, Marxist segment of feminism was too rigid and doctrinaire to reflect the needs and concerns of most women. In spite of the emphasis in rhetoric on the exploitation of working-class sisters on all fronts, I could not spot any of these women among the ranks. If the movement hopes to represent the needs of average women, it will have to speak a language which they can understand, and address itself to their concerns. In other words, get out of the socio-political ivory tower, and come down into the streets where we live.

In the meantime (this was Spring of 1970), social action was being planned in the form of an Abortion Caravan, culminating in the march and rally in Ottawa. I was enthusiastic about this co-ordinated effort by Women's Lib groups across Canada, and felt that here was something I could support unequivocally. The right of a woman to legal abortion affects me personally — affects women of all classes and political beliefs. Although I was a newcomer to the movement, and not involved in planning activities, I decided to take part in what would be my first public demonstration.

I set out to Ottawa feeling self-consciously militant, like a crusader on her first crusade! I arrived late, and went directly to the Parliament Buildings, where the rally had begun. How can I describe my feelings as I watched and listened to several hundred girls and women roaring their approval as speaker after speaker presented the case for woman's control of her own body, and cited the chronicles of humiliation and injustice suffered by women because they lacked this right? Delegates from the floor arose to bear witness, and I found tears in my eyes as I listened to a welfare recipient recount the indignities she suffered at the hands of welfare workers, male doctors and hospital committees, while desperately trying to obtain a therapeutic abortion.

I looked around at the women who packed the hall: mostly young, long-haired, and attired in what must be the obligatory uniform of jeans and Army surplus. On the whole, they were attractive, in their scrubbed youthful intensity. I spotted the odd butch type, some older women, in straight garb, and a few male supporters, whose presence somehow amused me. Women from welfare rights organizations were present and vocal, as were poor and average women. I was at first stunned as I heard the lusty cheers of "Right on!", and saw the raised fists which punctuated the speakers' remarks. I joined in the cheering, tentatively at first, then wholeheartedly. The raised fists made me uncomfortable for a while. The gesture was foreign to me, and I suppose I did not associate it with women. Yet, as the level of excitement caught me up, I found myself timidly making the gesture in response to a particularly effective speaker. After the first time it was easy, and I felt a sense of power and unity with the group mood, which was to carry me for the rest of the proceedings.

Afterwards we marched through the streets of Ottawa towards Trudeau's residence. I carried my first placard, and linking arms with fellow marchers, chanted slogans on the way. The vigor waned somewhat — it was a long walk — and the chants grew fainter, only to be started anew in an attempt to maintain the necessary level of excitement. When we finally arrived at the gates of Trudeau's residence, it was necessary to rush past a cordon of surprised policemen. After a brief token skirmish, we

182

gained entrance to the grounds, and I noted my own pleasurable excitement in 'storming the palace.'

Spirits were somewhat dampened when it became apparent that nobody was home, and no important personage was going to receive our presentation. We were further dampened by the rain, and it struck me how ridiculous this was, in a sense, squatting on the wet grass, spending rhetoric on policemen, and a hastily summoned aide of some sort. The crowd wanted to feel that it hadn't come for nothing, so the functionaries became the target of hostility perhaps better reserved for Trudeau, Turner, et al. "Male chauvinist pigs!" went the battle cry. Songs with obscene lyrics were sung. The policemen visibly blanched at hearing such utterances made by sweet girlish voices. The girls chortled gleefully.

I found myself operating on two levels. I was caught up in the catharsis of releasing anger and hostility at symbolic targets (they were still males, after all, and handy). At the same time, I watched the process incredulously, and wondered what the hell I was doing. Didn't the girls realize that their rhetoric was just that — this issue was not as simplistic as they were making it sound. In calling policemen pigs they were borrowing from another context; the term didn't have relevance here. These men weren't breaking heads, or perpetrating any brutalities whatsoever, only doing their policemen's job. Their worst sin seemed to be a reluctance to take us seriously, a bemusement about the whole situation. Perhaps this was the really infuriating thing: that since we were only women, even our capacity for lawbreaking wasn't taken seriously.

I felt currents of aggression around me, just awaiting a pretext to be released. There was a subliminal disappointment that the police hadn't misused their power, allowing us to be martyred. There was talk of staying on the grass in spite of the official warning that we were trespassing on private property and could be arrested — staying until an official met with us, or until we were bodily carted off to jail. Some diehards shouted their intention to remain, but were overruled by the wiser majority, who agreed that they could make better use of their time in planning strategy to fight another day. We trudged back to downtown Ottawa, unbloodied, wet, and in some strange way, purified.

And so ended my participation, for I had to return to Montreal to work, and thus missed the eventful Monday when some women chained themselves in the galleries and stopped the House.

I have reflected at some length on my reactions to that Saturday in Ottawa, for it put me in touch with a less familiar part of myself. Much of it can be attributed to crowd psychology, but that is not the point. I do not like all that I discovered in myself, but I will not deny it, for it affirms on the gut level what I knew intellectually.

For example, I harbour a special anger which rests in the depth of my being — an anger which has been fed by every frustration and insult which I have perceived as a female. This anger generally is not allowed to surface, or it appears disguised and diluted. It's a damn good feeling to let it out at long last, even though I realize that is only a stage which must be passed through.

I still haven't resolved all of my intellectual differences with the movement. It doesn't really matter. What does matter to me is that my participation focussed where I'm at emotionally as a women. I won't forget the shared anger, pride and love which I felt in the assembly in Ottawa. And which I continue to feel as I work with women in the campaign for abortion law repeal.

Participation in some aspect of Women's Liberation can put you in touch with your real feelings in a way that all the intellectual debates on women's role cannot. I only wish that some of the doubters and scoffers among my sisters could have such an experience. They might be surprised at what they learn about themselves.

THE FEMINIST REVOLUTION

by

Lin Green

As any woman who reads this will know, there is a state of revolution brewing. It will not be a process of gentle persuasion, nor a temporary revolt, nor will it consist of defiant token gestures. Although it is naturally the continuation of an ongoing process which began millennia ago, this time it will be an all-out effort to change the entire social structure a decaying structure based on false values.

I do not intend to take up space defining political ideologies. My opinions are of a human rather than of a political nature. Capitalist democracy supposedly defers to the will of the majority, although the will can obviously be bent for the right price. It may be argued that capitalism is based on self-interest and built on ego, communism being based on the concept of self-sacrifice for the good of all, which is intolerable. The latter point cannot be refuted, because man is not a sacrificial object to be disposed of for the 'common good.'

Neither is woman.

Yet women have not only been exploited by the capitalist system, but have been indoctrinated, conditioned and regulated to a degree found only in the totalitarian state. Capitalism has indeed worked, according to its principles, in the self-interest of *men* and supported by the ego of men. Women have had the evils of two opposing systems imposed upon them.

By a fractional margin, women form an oppressed majority of the population. Therefore they may rightfully be considered to comprise a revolutionary proletariat. Given the overall state of affairs in society, the enormous problems being faced, the agonizing frustration and desperation of a vast number of people, and most significantly the anger and political motivation of a growing number of women, it must be realized that ultimate political feminist revolution is inevitable. Moreover, it is right, proper, and in the natural order of things.

Women should be in the vanguard of social change, yet many women are in doubt as to the validity of the feminist premise. It is seen as a rationale for the avoidance of 'responsibility.' There is a serious connotation to the expression. Responsibility to whom? It must be remembered that one's first responsibility is to oneself. The denial of one's potential is a self-betrayal. Capitulation to the status quo is a betrayal.

The greatest single threat and disadvantage to women is fear of change. It is this fear alone which sends thousands of women cringing under the sanctimonious, sheltering umbrella of marriage. Fear of insecurity is a pathological phenomenon running rampant. Of course, women do not have a monopoly on feelings of insecurity and doubt. But the fact remains that they have more to lose by permitting themselves to be governed by such irrational fears.

We have been called the gentle sex. That is to say, we have remained at home to suckle the young while the men went to the wars. There have been men who possessed the same quality of gentleness, but that fact was brutally disregarded. Gentleness, it would appear, is no asset to man. Yet this quality, along with the virtues of compassion, humility, devotion and servility has been imposed upon woman, whether or not she was deserving of the honour. Qualities of human character have been rationed out according to gender. The sexes have been eound into their polarized straitjackets. The yawning chasm between them has nullified any attempt at understanding and true integration. Survival and reproduction of the species have been achieved only through truces rife with mistrust and vulnerability. The gentleness of the "gentle sex" has been manipulated by the aggressors, the war-makers, and by women themselves, in self-preservation and retaliation.

Aggression and hunger for power will not achieve peace. Masculine qualities have been responsible for all the wars in history. One might also consider the word patriotism and its masculine connotation.

Power in the wrong hands, to hackney a phrase, is deadly to all concerned. Power in the hands of an aggressor is imminent catastrophe. It follows, then, that only power combined with the feminine qualities of gentleness and compassion will begin to resolve the mess that man has gotten himself into.

What have men done to rectify past and present injustices? Several token gestures have been made by government, private industry, educational institutions, and on the individual level. These 'reforms' are announced with the peculiar air of one who is proclaiming his grand open-mindedness by deciding to bestow the privilege of human rights on a class of people who, he feels, are not quite ready for it, but who, he hopes, will respond favorably and shower him with the gratitude he so richly deserves. Bars, press clubs and the like are being desegregated and opened up. Job opportunities are expanding. Restrictions are falling away. The signs are promising. But are we to demonstrate our undying gratitude?

Cast a quick glance about, and note carefully the other nine companies out of ten that are *not* proclaiming aroused consciousness and liberation. Consider the rigid abortion laws that have *not* been repealed, the laws of coverture that have *not* been abolished, and perhaps most important of all, consider the prevailing attitudes, the barriers that remain among individual — the flag of male chauvinism that remains arrogantly hoisted. It remains there because it is woman who creates the breath of wind that brings it to life.

If real change is to be affected, the vicious cycle destroyed, a new element must appear in the behaviour of women: the element of universal sisterhood. Women must band together and proclaim

186

their allegiance to one another. By so doing, they will indeed be a force to contend with. Together, let us do away with feminine qualities that are results of a long period of conditioning. Let us do away with a vicious circle of misunderstandings.

Docility is not an admirable trait. Neither is cunning, in the sense that it is used by women. Dependence is a terrible burden upon the independent party. I would venture to say that these female characteristics are resented rather than appreciated by men. Women are held in contempt for the very qualities that they imagine to be desirable.

While it is true that men presently have a much higher individual and collective understanding of technology than women, it is also true that with proper education women could, within a generation, attain to the highest spheres of knowledge in this area.

The sciences and the trades, those fields most closely involved with the processes of technology, are profoundly male-oriented. Any form of creative innovation and construction is male territory. Engineering and electronics are obvious examples. In actual fact, one need look no further than the fact that the average woman is barely capable of performing the simplest mechanical tasks such as adjusting nuts, or faucet washers.

Education is at the core of the problem. It follows, then, that a drastic, not a piecemeal, change must be made in the educational system. However, women must take the initiative. It will not be easy, for they will be facing a locked door. The key is on the other side, that of the male establishment. The lock must be forced.

The educational structure, particularly where it involves females, must be radically overhauled. From their earliest years onward, young girls must be given opportunities that are presently non-existent. Talents and abilities must be recognized, encouraged and developed on a totally individual, non-sexist basis. Self-reliance and confidence should be emphasized.

"Vive la différence," say the French. Right. Without differences, life would be unbearable. We would exist in a vacuous no man's land of total equality. But there is a fine distinction to be made between differences of reason and differences of absurdity. Those of absurdity include many isms: racism, despotism, chauvinism, and sexism. What is valid and important is individual difference; the knowledge that every human being is unique. Notwithstanding the fact that they have been for so long, human beings cannot be categorically labelled and shelved like so many jam preserves in society's cupboard.

Much has been written, to date, of the social restrictions placed upon women, and of the effects of such restrictions. This, of course, is what Women's Liberation is all about. Not nearly as much has been said concerning the effects of society's restricting influences upon men. In any given society, male conditioning is the antithesis of whatever conditioning is inflicted upon the females of that society. Where females are not valued as a useful and constructive social force, the entire onus is heaved upon the males to create and maintain their society. In other words, where the burden of repression is placed on the female, the burden of responsibility is placed upon the male. Such responsibility cannot be undertaken indefinitely, and what is presently happening is the phenomenon of the responsible patriarchy teetering under the weight of its self-imposed obligations.

The only rational conclusion one can come to is that, rather than mulishly resisting the oncoming wave of anarchy regarding sex roles, men and women should yield to its influence and help in guiding it toward its ultimate destiny, which is the establishment of human liberation.

INTERNAL OPPRESSION

by

Judith B. Moody

What is women's liberation all about? It derives most of its strength from the fact that women want a real free choice — the ability to choose and define their own life pattern. We often hear: "you can do anything you want" or "you are free to marry or not," but those are not really free choices. Discriminatory hiring practices, unequal pay, sex-typing in jobs, unequal application of the law to women restrict all but the most determined to the socially approved choice: marriage without a career.

Two types of pressure limit the free choice of women: the type that is imposed on us by society, i.e. external oppression, and internal oppression or the oppression that is generated within

188

ourselves. The two types are inter-related and internal oppression could be considered as a response to external oppression. I would like to focus discussion on the second type of oppression which expresses itself most commonly as a form of self-hatred. However, a few brief comments about external oppression are in order.

The 'feminine mystique' in North America states that a woman's 'proper' place is in the home. This narrow definition of the female role is espoused by all persons in authority from the time a girl is born. It is expressed by the little four year old girl who tells her mother that she is going to be a nurse because girls are nurses and boys are doctors. This narrow vision of femininity is self-limiting to the individual woman because it leads her to expect less of herself, and limits her vision of her own potential as a human being.

One can not have a free choice when one is trapped by a narrow vision of one's self, one's capabilities and when one is filled with hatred for oneself and one's sex. This self-hatred, which is an expression of internal oppression, occurs in many forms: a general dislike for things considered feminine; identification with male aspirations; lack of consideration for and interest in women in your daily life; unwillingness to work with other women; alienation from or dislike for the female body and bodily functions; pigeon-holing other women according to their relationships with men. Self-hatred is destructive, in the sense that it feed and adds to the inadequacy that women already feel owing to their self-imposed and socially imposed limitations. It is reinforced by males, whose power is maintained by it.

The ability to get along with other women would be facilitated if we recognize that in part our difficulties stem from competition for men. We vie for men's attention because our chief source of power has been sexual in nature. This competition begins in the family with trying to attract your father's attention, is next transmitted to various possible marriageable suitors, and it extends into the business world in trying to curry the boss's favor. In sum, it is an integral part of the patriarchal society and is a strong force when women are economically or emotionally dependent on men.

This competition for men's attention is and will continue to be decisive as long as women define themselves *only* in a sexual manner. Meaningful relationships are readily achievable between women once this fierce competition for men stops. Women must learn to seek a personal identity through meaningful activity rather than concentrating on establishing a façade that is designed to

189

trap men more efficiently than the package the next woman designed.

Dislike for or alienation from the female body and bodily functions is something that has in large part been fostered on us by males. It has a long history and began in early cultures by segregation of women during menstruation because they were considered "unclean." It still persists in the general distaste for menstruation passed from mother to daughter — 'the curse' — and in such attitudes as "you can't have intercourse during your period." All the mysticism that surrounds "that time of the month" is false, unhealthy, and leads to a further negative factor in being female. Menstruation is just one of those things to be accepted, and certainly no more incapacitating for women than drinking habits, hypertension, ulcers, and virility fears are for men. It is true that women use menstruation as an excuse for many things, but again this is encouraged by men and it's an easy way to fall back on your sexual nature again when so little else is available.

The identification with male aspirations by women does not necessarily in itself have to be negative if one emphasizes the personal development of her own talents and abilities. It becomes negative when the professional woman takes on male attitudes towards women, especially chauvinistic attitudes, where she puts down other women or when she can no longer identify with the secretary who does her typing or the harried waitress who has been on her feet all day for minimal wages. It becomes negative when she does not give encouragement to the young struggling female lawyer, teacher or medical student with whom she has contact as a teacher or professional. It becomes negative when the professional woman does not fight in some way the discrimination that still exists against her and her position. She can sometimes easily forget that if discrimination exists against one of us, it exists against all of us. There is much that a woman who has made it can do, especially to help and encourage other women. The failure to do this is just again reinforcing their own self-hatred.

There are some successful professional women who fail to recognize the uniqueness of their own position. They say in effect "if I can do it, so can anyone else." These women are jealous of their own success, to the point of refusing to give of their experience to women who are just starting out. They are denying a basic part of their femininity in not recognizing their relationship with other women less successful than themselves.

190

The lack of consideration for and interest in other women is characteristic of women not only because of competitiveness for males, but because women have always placed their men and their families before themselves. It's difficult to analyze how this can change in the present pattern of marriage, unless women individually realize how much can be gained from seriously considering the women around them as human beings, as persons worth knowing. Women go through a process in seriously talking and listening to other women: one feels a tremendous lift in the sense of isolation that we all feel as human beings, I've heard many times ''but I thought I was the only woman who felt like that''; a sense of worth as a person is gained as others listen and take you seriously and you them; a beautiful feeling of solidarity is built up from shared e periences and ideas, which is the sisterhood many women speak about. Let's not minimize these things because they are *new* experiences for women and they should be enjoyed, savored, and continually re-experienced.

What does this all add up to? I think it is simply that we are our own worst enemies. Because the majority of women live with men and because men in a large part dominate our society, women have allowed themselves to be defined by them rather than trying to determine for womankind what it is to be female in all its many facets. The most fundamental and necessary change is for every woman to discover herself, and what she really wants from life, rather than taking any predetermined definition of what a woman ''should do'' in a given society in a given time.

This change will only come about when a woman looks upon herself as an *individual* with legitimate aspirations and no longer defines herself and other women by the status derived from relationships with men. This change means taking responsibility for yourself — entirely. This possibility for *real* freedom springs from the realization that you can define yourself in your own terms. Exercising this perogative requires courage to withstand intimidation and attempts by others to pigeon-hole your existence. That is why we women need each other.

WOMEN AND PERSONS

by

Christine Garside

I: Introduction

The basic premise of women's liberation is that women have the right to self-determination. This premise involves a commitment to two further statements, namely: 1) All persons have the right to self-determination; and 2) Women have been denied the right to self-determination. One could say that what it is to be a woman has been considered different in at least one important way from what it is to be a person.

II: All persons have the right to self-determination

Self-determination is to actively affirm a life goal for oneself and to actively engage in achieving that goal. It is essential that both kinds of activity take place for self-determination. For example, if one's life goal is adopted unconsciously even though a person actively engages in achieving that goal, it would not be sufficient for self-determination. An example of this might be a young girl who accepts society's mandate for marriage as her life goal and actively engages in finding a suitable husband. She would not have completed the first requirement for self-determination, viz. active affirmation of life goal. Specifically, she would not have chosen the goal in a way that involved previous reflection on alternatives. Active affirmation is different from enthusiastic unreflection. An example of failing to fulfil the second criterion for self-determination would be a woman who chooses to be a politician but is unable to actively pursue it because of her particular society's prejudice against women in politics. In this case, self-determination does not occur because she has not been able to actively engage in achieving her goal.

192

So when I say that all persons have the right to self-determination I mean that all persons have the right to actively affirm their life goals and to actively engage in achieving these goals. Two points must be made about self-determination before I continue. First, in this paper I am concerned only with self-determination not with self-fulfilment. The difference is that self-determination is a precondition for self-fulfilment. Self-fulfilment is dependent upon several other factors which remain to some extent out of the control of the individual. For example, to be fulfilled in life one must have deep and long lasting friendships, a sense of the value of one's life work, mental and physical health, freedom from poverty, and so on. In this paper I will not discuss factors relating to self-fulfilment but will instead limit myself to one pre-condition for fulfilment, viz. self-determination. It is *possible* to have self-determination without self-fulfilment and *impossible* to have self-fulfilment without self-determination.

My second point about self-determination is that it is an on-going process. Life goals are not chosen once and for all. On the contrary, they are constantly being rechosen. While I will limit myself in this paper to discussing self-determination at any particular time in life, it is understood that this process is and should be a continuous one throughout an entire life. A life goal then is a specific time chosen through reflection which gives a meaning and structure to everything we do.

Immediately we face another contentious issue: the question of right vs. privilege. There is a paradox at the core of the right to self-determination. Specifically, in order to justify a right to self-determination one must appeal to human nature; and in order to explain human nature one must include self-determination.

There are ways of resolving this paradox. We could say that all persons have the potentiality for self-determination by virtue of being born human but that only those who actualize this, i.e. those who actively live a life of continuous self-determination are persons in the full sense.[1] This resolution is unsatisfying, however, in that it leads to all sorts of other problems like the difference between un-self-determined persons and the rest of nature, the lack of sensitivity to shared human characteristics, and so on. The fact is that persons live with different levels of self-determination. We are a person precisely because we have the right to self-determination and we have that right precisely because we are a person. There is no satisfactory resolution to this paradox of the right to self-determination.

Historically this right has been abdicated frequently by groups in society and by individuals in a group. In these cases the abdication has often occurred unconsciously and occasionally consciously. In general, however, the person or group which has received the abdication has then incorporated it until the right to self-determination for the abdicator was seen as a privilege. For anyone trying to win back their birthright it became a struggle which invariably led back to the central question: What is it to be a person? Aristotle believed that only a few male persons should be self-determined, Kierkegaard believed that all male persons should be self-determined, and today we find a different approach altogether. Those who had abdicated their right to self-determination and who demand it back are doing so for everyone — female as well as male persons. This right in no way can be seen as a privilege extended to any group or individual in a society; it is the birthright of any child coming forth from its mother's womb. To ask why this should be so is to ask why a baby must take that first breath of air. Once you have tasted the sweetness and pain of this birthright no rational argument could ever persuade you to abdicate it again.

Someone might wish to argue with me at this point that my appeal to experience is just not enough to prove that the right to self-determination is a birthright. She or he could say that I am appealing to some ineffable self-evident experience which leaves little else to be said. I would answer that this criticism is correct. In the end there is little more than can be said. Of course I could point out that the other alternative, namely that the right of self-determination is *not* a birthright leads to some very unfortunate consequences. Then we might examine some of these consequences together. One such consequence involves the problem of one person deciding what is good for another. The practice of binding the feet of Chinese female babies before a girl could conceivably choose the other alternative ends up with a deformed adult incapable of running or walking freely. Similarly, I could argue that the practice of programming young girls to abdicate self-determination frequently ends up with deformed women incapable of full self-determination. Here, however, my critic and I would eventually have to return to the question of what it is to be a person and there would be no further court of appeal.

There is also another way to object to my appeal to self-evidence in the case of the right to self-determination for all persons. This time my critic might say, using the same line of reasoning as above, that there are some very unfortunate consequences of my

194

claiming that women have the right to self-determination. They might use the familiar example: If women can be self-determined then what happens to the children?[2] Here again I must point out that I am not discussing the responsibilities of self-determination but merely the principle that all persons have the right to it.

The right to self-determination can not be established by an appeal to consequences in either direction. It must be based on the criteria for being a person. To argue from consequences is to place the cart before the horse. Consequences are important not in establishing self-determination as a right but in considering the rights of others; and this leads us into the larger problem of self-fulfilment.

III: Women have been denied the right to self-determination

The distinguished philosopher Immanuel Kant had the following observations to make about women:

> All the other merits of a woman should unite solely to enhance the character of the beautiful, which is the proper reference point; and on the other hand, among the masculine qualities the sublime clearly stands out as the criterion of his kind. All judgments of the two sexes must refer to this criteria ... unless one wants to disguise the charming distinction that nature has chosen to make between the two sorts of human being. For here it is not enough to keep in mind that we are dealing with human beings; we must also remember that they are not all alike.[3]

The crucial point here and the one I want to devote the remainder of the paper to is the claim that women and men are different *in respect to* their right to self-determination. For Kant the sublime and the noble are meant for man. Specifically, for a woman to seek after the noble is to give up what she is and to try to become a man.

> Deep meditation and a long-sustained reflection are noble, but difficult, and do not well befit a person in whom unconstrained charms should show nothing else than a beautiful nature. Laborious learning or painful pondering, even if a woman should greatly succeed in it, destroy the merits that are proper to her sex ... A woman who has a head full of Greek ... might as well even have a beard; for perhaps that would express more obviously the mien of profundity for which she strives.[4]

This view could be ignored if it were not so generally accepted by western male philosophers. In another paper I have shown that Aristotle and Kierkegaard maintained precisely the same position.[5] If you compare what they claim is necessary for a person to be good with what they claim is possible for a woman, the result is that a woman can not ultimately be good. Another way of saying this is that for a woman to attempt to achieve the practical wisdom of Aristotle, to live the true Christianity of Kierkegaard, or to follow the categorical imperative of Kant is to attempt to become a man.

In all three of these philosophers the crucial point is the relation between self-determination and reflection. For Kant, "Her philosophy is not to reason, but to sense"[6]; for Aristotle her virtue is "not wisdom, but only true opinion"[7]; and for Kierkegaard "No woman is able to endure a dialectical reduplication, and everything Christian has a dialectical element in it."[8] Since reflection on oneself and on one's life as a whole is an essential part in actively choosing a life goal it follows that women can not be self-determined. For these philosophers the right to self-determination extends only to men.

It is my claim that this view is fundamentally wrong because it confused the activity of self-determination with the product. If we examine this confusion in terms of reflection it can be expressed as a mixing of the faculty of reflection and the content of the reflection. Both women and men have the same faculty by virtue of being human, but what it is that is reflected on is different in many ways by virtue of their being female or male. Similarly, both men and women are able to be self-determined by virtue of being persons; what kind of self-determined person they will be, however, will differ because the basic data of their determination is different. This means that women will always be different from men as the result of self-determination because we differ in physical structure, we differ in our present social experience, we differ in our inherited past and so on.

I suspect that it was in some part the fear of loss of polarity between the sexes which led to the traditional denial of self-determination for women. This fear, however, is groundless for a true polarity will emerge when women and men press forward in active self-determination. It might be helpful to look at one philosopher who recognized that self-determination was not a defining male characteristic in order to discover how it was that he justified this view.

Two major problems jump to the surface when one first attempts to come to terms with Plato's views on women. The first is the diversity of contemporary interpretations of Plato on women and the second is the seeming contradiction about women found in the dialogues themselves. Needless to say, the first problem is directly related to the second.

Although there are many examples of the first problem I will limit the discussion to one — Simone de Beauvoir. In *The Second Sex* there are only three references to Plato, but each one takes a different aspect to emphasize. In one she is discussing the feelings of superiority men have had historically:

> The first among the blessings for which Plato thanked the gods that he had been created free, not enslaved; the second, a man, not a woman.[9]

In another reference she mentions his vision of the emancipation of women:

> Plato envisioned a communal regime and promised women an autonomy in it such as they enjoyed in Sparta.[10]

And finally she refers to the essential bisexuality of humanity:

> However, even if a man can subjectively go through erotic experiences without women being present, she is objectively implied in his sexuality: as Plato says in the myth of Androgynes, the organism of the male supposes that of the female.[11]

It is surprising that a philosopher like de Beauvoir could rest content with such a superficial account of Plato on women. Anyone who has read the *Symposium* carefully knows that Plato is making fun of the myth of Androgynes. Aristophanes, in recording this myth, states that there were originally three sexes: man-man, man-woman, and woman-woman.[12] After these were split the descendants searched for their counterpart. There is no doubt that the woman-man union was seen as inferior to the man-man union and superior to the woman-woman union. In the light of this de Beauvoir's use of this myth to support the claim of the inherent bi-sexuality of persons is suspect.[13]

However, the kind of ambiguity reflected in de Beauvoir is found in many contemporary women when it comes to Plato. On the one hand, they want to applaud his visionary belief that women should be given equal opportunities in society, that the family structure must be changed to allow this equality, and so on. On the other hand, they sense a hatred of women in his views on homosexuality, with his adoration of ideal women coupled with his exclusion of real women.[14]

The next question to be faced is whether this conflict is inherent

197

in Plato or is there some consistent doctrine about women through-out the dialogues. The answer to this question depends upon the importance one gives to the myths Plato includes in his dialogues. Friedländer claims that Plato uses myths on three levels:

> On the first level, the myth stands at the threshold of the Socratic world ... on the second level, Socrates himself takes hold of the myth ... on the third level, Socrates is seized by divine mania.[15]

The important point about Friedländer's insights into the use of myth in Plato is that when we are struggling to reach an understanding of the true view of Plato on a particular problem we must penetrate the third and second level of myths. In the present case where we seek to find his view on women we must turn to the myths of the origin of women and men particularly in the *Timaeus* and the *Phaedrus*.

In the *Phaedrus* we learn that the soul is immortal (245), that it has a vision of the divine (247), that if it is not strong enough it goes through a process of rebirth (248), and that in this process during the first birth it takes on the body of a man. The *Timaeus* adds to our knowledge of this process as regards women:

> Of the men who came into the world, those who were cowards or led unrighteous lives may with reason be supposed to have changed into the nature of women in the second generation. (91)

Plato had a vision of the person which was separate from sex. The soul was neither female nor male. One was first a person, then during the first birth a man, and during the second possibly a woman.

It is important to understand the main point Plato is making here before we discuss his views on the liberation and education of women. What it is to be a person *exists prior to* what it is to be a woman or a man. Their original nature is the same.[16]

The difficulty is that a woman reading the *Timaeus* could easily come away with the impression that Plato hates women. In addition to this premise that women were previously cowards or unrighteous men we find in this particular dialogue another view which is equally outdated and incorrect. He says:

> For the present we have only to conceive of three natures; first, that which is in process of generation; secondly, that in which the generation takes place; and thirdly, that of which the thing generated is a resemblance. And we may liken the receiving principle to a mother, and the source or spring to a father, and the intermediate nature to a child. (50)

198

It would be easy on first reading to conclude from this that he is saying women or mothers should be like matter — viz., formless. On closer inspection, however, this conclusion dissolves. Plato along with his contemporaries misunderstood conception and believed that the woman only provided a receptacle for the male seed. The dual aspect of conception — that new life needs two sources — has been a discovery of modern genetics. In his attempt to explain the metaphysical categories of form and matter Plato drew upon a common misconception. What he meant by source or form and receiving principle or matter still remains tenable even though our understanding of mother and father have changed. We must be careful not to argue from the example or the analogy to the underlying metaphysical categories. Unfortunately, too many philosophers have done so to the detriment of women. For example, with Aristotle the metaphysical categories of form and matter have become prescriptive for women and men in a way Plato avoided by his expression "we may liken ..."

> The female always provides the material, the male that which fashions it, for this is the power that we say they each possess, and this is what is meant by calling them male and female.[17]

In short Plato did not tie the nature of women or man down to common beliefs. He used them where applicable to draw out his metaphysical presuppositions. If these beliefs were to change Plato could easily have changed his examples. The reason for his flexibility is, I believe, his underlying thesis about what it is to be a person.

We are now in a position to come to terms with Plato's views on self-determination for women. In the *Republic* Socrates asks Glaucon:

> You will admit that the same education which makes a man a good guardian will make a woman a good guardian; for their original nature is the same? (456)

If women and men were born in a particular body because of their previous life and if the purpose of life is to become progressively enlightened about truth then it follows that all people should receive the best possible education, that all should be encouraged to seek wisdom, that all should be able to live the kind of life which reflects the degree of wisdom attained. In the *Republic* and in the *Laws* Plato develops his views on how we can best become reunited with that from which we have been separated. How can we return to the divine?

Since for Plato all evil is due to ignorance, the purpose of a good society should be to rid its members of as much ignorance as possible. To know the good is to do the good. And since the amount of good or evil in a society is directly related to the number of good or evil people in the society, it follows that *all* members of that society should seek to get rid of ignorance.[18]

> And I further affirm, that if these things are possible, nothing can be more absurd than the practice which prevails in our own country, of men and women not following the same pursuits with all their strength and with one mind, for thus the state, instead of being a whole, is reduced to a half.[19]

Women must receive the same education as men for two reasons: first because they are persons and second because not to educate them is to weaken the state. The second reason is reflected in Plato's views on genetics as well as in his concern with socialization. In the *Republic* the most perfect should mate together most and the least perfect least.[20]

It is clear now that women must be given the same opportunities for growth in a good society as men; and as is well known Plato even believed women should be allowed to be guardians of the state if they had the right character.[21]

> Men and women alike possess the qualities which make a guardian; they differ only in their comparative strength or weakness.[22]

So what appeared at first glance to be a contradictory view on the nature of woman turns out to be quite consistent. To summarize briefly, Plato believed that all persons exist independently from and prior to their bodies, that some are born as men, some reborn as women, that the purpose of life is to achieve as much perfection as possible in order to escape the cycle of rebirth, that to achieve this purpose all persons in a society should be given the best education and the same opportunities for self-determination. In view of our major task in this paper we can safely say that Plato would agree with both statements: 1) All persons have the right to self-determination and 2) Women have been denied the right to self-determination. Of course, he sets definite limits to self-determination which depend upon self-fulfilment and the fulfilment of society as a whole, but this is another issue.

For Plato the *reason* women should have the right to self-determination is because they are persons. Even though he would agree that in general women are inferior to men he none-the-less realizes that they are not different as far as the right to self-

200

determination should be concerned. For Plato this equality is due to the belief in the pre-existence of the soul. We are now in the peculiar position of discovering that the only philosopher who stands out before the nineteenth century as agreeing with my thesis that women and men are alike in respect to their right to self-determination justifies his claim on the more basic belief in the pre-existence of the soul. For Aristotle, Kant or Kierkegaard there was never any question of a person existing as devoid of sexuality — for them there were only women and men. And in this I would be forced to agree.

Is it necessary to have recourse to a prior bodyless state in order to allow for equal status for self-determination? The answer to this is negative, although there is no question that the body plays a central role in the tradition of denial of self-determination for women.

In the essay *The Subjection of Women*, J. S. Mill examines what he takes to be the basis for this denial.

> The adoption of this system of inequality never was the result of deliberation, or forethought, or any social ideas, or any notion whatever of what conduced to the benefit of humanity or the good order of society. It rose simply from the fact that from the very earliest twilight of human society, every woman (owing to the value attached to her by men, combined with her inferiority in muscular strength) was found in a state of bondage to some man. Laws and systems of polity always begin by recognizing the relations they find already existing between individuals. They convert what was a mere physical fact into a legal right.[23]

For Mill the person is not a pre-existing soul and yet we find a recognition of woman's right to self-determination. The body is central to the definition of the individual, but size or comparative physical strength becomes irrelevant. Men and women are persons *because* they can be self-defined. To be an individual is to employ all the faculties available.

> He who lets the world, or his own portion of it, choose his plan of life for him, has no need of any other faculty than the ape-like one of imitation. He who chooses his plan for himself, employs all his faculties.[34]

And it goes without saying that for Mill women and men have the same faculties. They sense, they imagine, they reflect, they choose; in short they are able to be self-determined.

> He who would rightly appreciate the worth of personal independence as an element of happiness, should consider the value he himself

puts upon it as an ingredient of his own ... let him rest assured that whatever he feels on this point, women feel in a fully equal degree.[25]

IV: Conclusion

In this paper I have demonstrated that the right to self-determination can not be justified by an appeal to consequences — that it is its own justification. Furthermore, this right is either applicable to all persons or to none. The only reason why it is necessary to refer to women's liberation in this context is because the right to self-determination has usually been denied to women. Liberation is necessary from the mistaken belief that men are unique by virtue of their ability to reflect and women by their ability to intuit.[26] Similarly, liberation is necessary from the confused claim that when a woman begins to assert her ability for self-determination she is becoming a man.[27] I have shown how this view is mistaken — that it focuses on faculties and activities instead of content and product.

Further, it was seen that while Plato understood that women should be self-determined he did not give a foundation for it which is acceptable to the twentieth century mind. Mill, on the other hand, openly appealed to a common ground of human experience saying that what men see as a right for themselves women equally desire — unless, of course, they have been deformed by their experience to such an extent that they willingly abdicate what is rightfully theirs.

Finally, I would like to reiterate my belief that there is no need to fear loss of polarity when women do achieve liberation on the level of self-determination. Unfortunately, even many of the women writing today on the subject seem to think otherwise. They believe that 'after the revolution' there will exist only individuals.[28] There is no way that women can ever become identical to men.[29] Nor is there any reason why they should desire to do so. The heritage and experience of women is as rich as the heritage and experience as men; and once women recognize their right to self-determination and release their creative energies into the world this will be obvious.

1. Sartre takes this approach in *Being and Nothingness*. "Human reality is not something which exists first in order afterwards to lack this or that; it exists first as a lack and in immediate, synthetic connection with what it lacks." *Being and Nothingness*, Hazel Barnes trans., Philosophical Library, New York, p. 89.

2. Margaret Mead argues this way in *Male and Female* and in recent press interviews.

3. Immanuel Kant, *Of the Beautiful and Sublime,* Goldthwait trans., University of California Press, Berkeley, 1965, pp. 76-7.

4. *Ibid.*, p. 78.

5. Garside, ''Can a Woman be Good in the Same Way as a Man?'' in *Dialogue,* Canadian Philosophical Review, Vol. X, 1971, No. 3, pp. 534-544. My arguments in the present paper presuppose the validity of the conclusions reached in the previous one. Therefore, I will not present the arguments for this position again.

6. Kant, *op. cit.,* p. 79.

7. Aristotle, 1277b 28.

8. Kierkegaard, *The Last Years* (Journals, 1853-55), The Fontana Library, 1968, p. 69.

9. Simone de Beauvoir, *The Second Sex,* Parshley trans., Bantam Books, U.S.A., p. xxi.

10. *Ibid.*, p. 103.

11. *Ibid.*, p. 150.

12. Plato, *Symposium,* 190.

13. It is interesting to note that Karl Stern in *The Flight from Woman* makes the same mistake. See *The Flight From Woman,* Farrar, Straus and Giroux, New York. 1965, p. 11.

14. In the Symposium we find Socrates being taught about wisdom and love by Diotima while the flute girl joins the other women outside the gathering. There is some dispute, however, about Diotima being a mythical figure as Mary Beard points out in *Woman as Force in History,* Collier Books, New York, pp. 324-5. Even if there were women philosophers they certainly were not included in Socrates' gatherings.

15. Paul Friedlander, *Plato, An Introduction,* Hans Meyerhoff trans., Harper Torchbooks, New York, pp. 207-8.

16. Plato, *Republic,* 456.

17. Aristotle 738b 20.

18. Plato *Republic* 456.

19. Plato *Laws* 560.

20. Plato *Laws* 775.

21. Plato *Republic* 455.

22. Plato *Republic* 456.

23. J. S. Mill, ''The Subjection of Women'' in *On Liberty, Representative Government, The Subjection of Women,* Oxford University Press, London, 1969, pp. 431-2.

24. *Ibid.*, p. 78.

25. *Ibid.*, p. 543.

26. Stern *Op. Cit.* The absurdity of this position is carried throughout the book in which he castigates men for fleeing from intuition.

27. As mentioned previously — both Kant and Kierkegaard made this extreme claim.

28. Shulamith Firestone is particularly guilty of this in *The Dialectic of Sex,* Bantam Books, 1970. It is not surprising that she ties this view to a total rejection of female biological experience.

29. Kate Millett in *Sexual Politics* recognizes this and calls for a re-examination of the desirability of some of the traits considered as exclusively masculine or feminine not a rejection of sexual polarity altogether. Doubleday and Company, Inc., 1970, p. 62.

The above article is being published with the permission of the philosophy department of the State University College, Fredonia, N.Y. The article won first prize in an essay contest on the philosophical bases of women's liberation, sponsored by that university.

THE ROYAL
COMMISSION REPORT

I AM MY SISTER'S KEEPER

by

Jean McIllwrick

Over the years the women of Canada have been well served by a few women who cared about the lack of rights for the women in this country. Even our government has done its part by appointing the Royal Commission on the Status of Women in Canada. The members of this Commission have drawn up a list of recommendations which they feel will improve the conditions for women in Canada. It is up to us, all of us, to study these recommendations and to pressure the Government to implement as many of them as we are in agreement with. The recommendations will not become fact unless pressure is brought to bear. There are many women who feel that their position does not need to be improved, but this does not mean that all Canadian women are so fortunate. It is important that women show concern for others of their sex. The time has come for us to change the question: "Am I my brother's keeper?" to a firm commitment: I am my sister's keeper.

WOMEN IN POLITICS

by

Catherine Shiff

The distance between the position of women and that of men in our society is no more apparent than on the political scene. Representation of women in Parliament, provincial legislatures and municipal councils is almost negligible, and as indicated in the Commission's Report, more so in Quebec than elsewhere in Canada. There is no doubt that women's self image must be enhanced in terms of their potential capabilities, talents and ability to participate and contribute to the political life of their community and their country. There is a fear that lurks in the hearts of men that the dutiful wife will no longer accept her 'natural' station in life if she is to assume her rightful place in a Just Society.

The famous matriarchy of North American women is a myth perpetuated on TV screens and psychiatrist's couches. They lag further behind men in economic, professional, academic and political life than the women of other countries at whom the accusation has never been levelled. All the stories about husbands taking out the garbage and minding the children are really diversionary tactics. It is precisely women's exclusion from administrative, economic and political leadership which results in the popular assertion that they are a power behind the scenes. And the imbalance is never felt more than when the wife of a politician is covered in the women's section of the press as having a decorous role without which her husband could never succeed. Would it not be better if the female candidate ran her own campaign assuming full responsibility for her acts and beliefs and finally winning an office for herself? It is about time that our women began to recognize this inequality.

A feminine revolution has been under way for some time now,

demographic in its nature, if you will. The life span of women has been considerably extended, they outlive men and are consequently more numerous among the over-forties, they marry younger, bear children in their early youth and as a result the period of their lives devoted to maternity in relation to total life expectation is shrinking. From now on the longest phase of their lives will be that which follows the completion of a family.

It is paradoxical in our society that the women who participate to such a negligible degree in political careers can participate to such a large extent in voluntary organizations which pursue civic aims and have an important influence on local politics. They carry out vigorous campaigns to get out the voters but always within the framework of strict neutrality. Why can't we mobilize our human resources — a committee of representatives from various women's groups to support a qualified woman candidate — on the local level? It is the woman who is closest to the scene and there is no question of her mobility. She recognizes the problems and has the talent to view them on a long term basis. Why is there such a lack of interest in municipal affairs from whence stem the land speculation and the exploitation of our natural resources? And isn't the mother the most likely one to be concerned with the educational needs of the community?

A grounding on the local level will be a beginning for a future political career. Hopefully, the financing for such a campaign will come from the party or public funds. All too often a woman may be without resources to launch any kind of adequate campaign. With the support of women, we may produce more women candidates in the political arena. No political party should receive the support of women voters unless its platform contains an equal rights for women plank.

I would hope for and look to the press for a fair coverage of women in politics. Aside from the women's section in the newspaper the woman politician is very often denigrated. In the recent Montreal Island municipal elections the caption in the Montreal *Star* read, "Voters Turn Thumbs Down on Women." This was not a true reflection of what really happened. Most of the candidates, while not winning the election, received substantial amounts of the votes.

The Province of Quebec is about the only province without a human rights code. It is to be hoped that the one in the offing, as promised by the Justice Minister, will contain a provision that will not deny equality of rights under the law because of sex. There are intangible psychological benefits ensuing from this guarantee in forging a new solidarity among women that fosters self confidence and the courage to use rights already theirs but not claimed because of fears.

In order to give visibility and priority to the ultimate goal of equality for women, the Federal government should establish an office of Women's Rights. This would offer concrete evidence that the government is committed to action on behalf of women's rights. It would be the task of this office to inform leaders of all branches of government, business, labor, education etc. on the nature and scope of the problem of sex discrimination, striving to enlist their support in working toward improvement.

More women should be appointed to positions of top responsibility in the Federal government. Appointments must be based on merit rather than sex. We must concentrate on increasing the percentage of women elected, only then will the prestige of the female politician rise and the political education of our women will improve.

In the last analysis it is all up to us. We can no longer confine our thoughts to our own household, nor our sympathies to our own creed, color or even community. We have to identify with that group of women who are trying to look beyond their own concerns and work toward a better world.

THE STATUS OF WOMEN IN CANADA

by

Lucia Kowaluk

There is no longer any reason for Canadians to reject the basic premise of the Women's Lib position, which is that by every measure most valued in our society — money, authority, education, freedom of choice, accomplishment — women are in an inferior position compared to men. *The Report of the Royal Commission on the Status of Women*, in the making three and a half years, and published in September, 1970, holds page after graph after chart of information to make squirm a society which in its rhetoric holds dear the values of equality and individual freedom. The chapters on women in the economy, the education of women and the poverty of women give facts which are shocking.

Some examples: Women represent one third of the labour force which is one third of the female population old enough to work; yet of all income reported in 1967, women received $7.5 billion or about 20%. (p. 21) Most of that was from pensions and alimony; of earned income, women received 4.5%. A third of the labour force received 4.5% of its income! Women hold less than 1% of the top corporate positions in Canada. (p. 28) Graphed by average yearly earnings, in managerial jobs men earn between two and three times as much as women; it is the same in sales jobs. In professional jobs, men earn nearly twice as much; in service and recreation the same situation prevails. Whereas there are two and three times as many women in all types of work in the salary ranges below $6,000 a year, the ratio abruptly changes as the salary rises, and in the bracket above $10,000 — in the professions, for example — the ratio is 17 men to one woman. (p. 62-3)

Although the number of women enrolled in university is rising, women still receive only one third of all the B.A. degrees and less than one fifth of the advanced degrees. (p. 168) The poverty figures are equally shocking. When the head of a family is a woman, she is three times as likely as a man to have an income of $3,000 or less, four times as likely to have an income of $2,000 or less and six times as likely, $1,000 or less. (p. 322) According to 1967 data, the average income of all women heads of families was $2,536; the average income of male heads was $5,821. (p. 320) Elderly women are even worse off — thousands of them living alone. In 1967, the average annual income for all women 65 and over was $1,596, for all similar men, $3,044. (p. 326)

The figures go on and on. Not only do the statistics cry out about the very fundamental insecurity and inferiority of women in this society, but the quotes both from any of the 469 briefs read by the Commission, and from the Commissioners themselves describe what this inferior and insecure position does to women. "Traditionally the economy has been a man's world and practice today perpetuates that tradition. Such a world provides fertile grounds for nourishing the belief that women's inferior financial position is synonymous with an incapacity to make important financial decisions. And one of the unfortunate consequences of such a long-standing belief is that women themselves fall victim to it. It is not surprising then that many women lack confidence in their ability to handle financial affairs or to play a useful part in setting corporate policies." (p. 30) Under the section on "Unpaid Work" the Commissioners write, "As long as most unpaid work (includes all housework, help in family business, and volunteer work) is performed by women, *their status* will largely be determined by the *economic* importance society attaches to such work" (p. 32 emphasis mine). And later on page 52,

Earlier we touched briefly on the financial dependency of housewives which results from their production of goods and services without pay. Perhaps more than anything else, this is responsible for the present position of women. It can have a destructive effect both on the housewife and on daughters who, because they take the housewife's state of dependency as a matter of course, may see little purpose in preparing for financial independence themselves. More than this, the fairly common state of women's financial dependency follows those seeking to escape it through paid work. In the business world, the belief still remains with some employers that women should be paid less because they have husbands to support them. One of the most destructive features of financial dependency is that it can undermine the confidence of the housewife in her own ability to make decisions not only within the home but also in the outside world. In a society in which income is one of the factors influencing status, she is already at a disadvantage. If she has a dependent role in the family, she will question her ability to be a leader in other areas where she will be competing with men. And if men are accustomed to holding financial power within the family, they are unlikely to assume that women are able to wield such power outside the home. (p. 52)

But some women do reach senior positions. Having gone through the mill, what do they think about the comparative opportunities of women and men? We asked this question of a group of women who had 'made the grade'. They generally agreed that women had fewer opportunities for advancement than men but that not all the blame lies with employers. They felt that the smaller proportion of women with university degrees severely handicaps women as a group, and that the breaks in most women's employment often deprive them of valuable experience and put them out of touch with current developments. They considered women less likely than men to increase their educational status after leaving school or to take advantage of training courses. They also agreed that many women are strongly motivated and well-qualified and that even these women find it hard to reach senior levels. As one woman put it: "The natural inclination is to pick the man so that he (the employer) has no reason for picking the woman unless she has better qualifications,'' (p. 96)

In the chapter on 'Education,' space is devoted to the motivation of girls for schooling:

> While they are still in school, girls tend to have low occupational expectations, even when they express interest in more challenging fields. Responses to a recent survey based on a national sample showing, for example, that although only 18% of fourth-year highschool girls preferred sales and clerical careers, 32% seemed to assume that they would eventually work in these fields. According to the results of the survey, the careers boys want are closer to those they expect to have. (p. 180)

And the Commission's description of poverty is both accurate and moving:

> Poverty is to be without sufficient money, but it is also to have little hope for better things. It is a feeling that one is unable to control one's destiny, that one is powerless in a society that respects power. The poor have very limited access to means of making known their situation and their needs. To be poor is to feel apathy, alienation from society, entrapment, hopelessness and to believe that whatever you do will not turn out successfully. To be poor is to feel deprived of the means of attaining even the most elementary things that others take for granted. According to recent investigations, it appears that there are few 'voluntary poor'; that on the contrary most of the poor are ready to seize appropriate job opportunities when these are available. '. . . Some recent research suggests that the aspirations of the poor for economic opportunities and a middle-class style of life, may be very strong, and that the desire to participate in a productive way in our society is more often frustrated than lacking.' The poor are hindered by a 'high incidence of inadequate skills and education, a lack of knowledge about how to seek out and exploit job opportunities, sickness and repeated thwarting of employment aspirations.' (p. 311)
>
> The harsh consequences of poverty are compounded for women. If a woman is among the 'working poor' she knows the frustrations and disappointments, the sense of inferiority, which are the inevitable result of working hard for little return . . . The feelings of helplessness and self-depreciation which are one of the most serious aspects of poverty may be hers in double measure. (p. 315)

Some of these descriptions apply to all Canadian women, all of them apply to some. Some Canadian women are more free of the negative self-image than others, but they always have a gnawing feeling that they have to fight hard to hold that freedom. Some Canadian women are financially secure and comfortable because they are cared for, but they are often, what Germaine

213

Greer has brilliantly pointed out, female eunuchs: not unhappy or restless, but without the drive for and the excitement of achievement that humankind has held as one of its most precious attributes.

The Royal Commission Report is far more detailed than the highlights mentioned here. The chapter on the economy spends pages citing discrimination, not only in private business and labour unions, but in government service as well. It also tries to give some way of measuring housework into the GNP. The chapter on the family is concerned with the legal status of women both married and single, and proposes reforms in marriage and divorce laws, as well as protection for children. A large section is devoted to day care, the area that nearly everyone in and out of Women's Lib agrees is an essential addition to our present urban life. There are chapters on tax reforms to make more equitable the taxation of working mothers, on women in politics, immigration and criminal law. As a description of the status of women in Canada, the Commission Report is a valuable document and an essential handbook for the people who want to use the facts to begin an analysis for change.

So now — what to do about it? The Commission itself has presented 167 recommendations, stated at the appropriate places throughout the report, and repeated all together at the end. These recommendations deal almost entirely with proposals for new laws and government policies. This is the frame of reference that the Commission has given itself, although the Report makes it clear in a number of places that laws are only a beginning and a partial solution.

> Perhaps no prejudice in human society is so deeply imbedded or so little understood. To create equality it will be necessary to create a totally new climate, a totally new frame of reference against which every question affecting women can be assessed. Such a transformation will not follow the publication of one report. It will be achieved only as a consequence of a continuing study of the position of women in society and continuous efforts to secure justice and equal opportunity. (p. 389)

There can be no question as to where the sympathies of the Commissioners lie; the data have clearly convinced them that the status of women in Canada is unjust. In a preface dealing with criteria and principles, they state four "givens": "that women should be free to choose whether or not to take employment outside their homes . . . . that the care of children is a responsibility to be shared by the mother, the father and society . . . that society has a responsibility for women because of pregnancy and child-

214

birth, and special treatment related to maternity will always be necessary ... that in certain areas women will for an interim period require special treatment to overcome the adverse effects of discriminatory practices." (p. xii)

The recommendations on a number of the most timely and controversial questions bear mention. Regarding abortion, the Commission recommends amending the Criminal Code "to permit abortion by a qualified medical practitioner on the sole request of any woman who has been pregnant for 12 weeks or less ... [and] by a qualified practitioner at the request of a woman pregnant for more than 12 weeks if the doctor is convinced that the continuation of the pregnancy would endanger the physical or mental health of the woman, or if there is a substantial risk that if the child were born, it would be greatly handicapped, either mentally or physically." (p. 286)

The Commission recommends the complete abolition of special protective labour legislation governing women, a recommendation which angered many labour leaders but which the Commission defends on the grounds that protective legislation should apply to all employees if there are dangers to health or dignity. (p. 89) They recommend unemployment insurance payments (under an amended Act) for maternity leave up to 18 weeks. They also recommend "that (a) both the Canada and Quebec Pension Plans be amended so that the spouse who remains at home can participate in the Plan, and (b) the feasibility be explored of crediting to the spouse remaining at home a portion of the contributions made by the employer on the employed spouse's behalf, and on an optional basis, permitting the spouse at home to contribute as a self-employed worker." (p. 40) This recommendation followed several pages of discussion on the role, work and status of the housewife, an area which the Commission recognized as crucial when it wrote, "Probably the most frequently voiced dissatisfaction of married women who work in the home is the low status society gives to housework when they themselves feel the work they perform there is important to the family and society." (p. 37)

In the area of taxation, a proposal to balance what the Commission believes is an unfair advantage to childless wives who work at home against wives who work outside the home, is a sharp reduction in the husband's deduction for a "dependent" wife (she is not a dependent but gives in labour and services at least what she receives in food and shelter), and sharp increase in deductions for children who are in reality dependents. (p. 303)

The minority report by John Humphreys presents a very valid criticism of this tax proposal by raising the problem of population explosion. At a time when the whole world is and should be concerned with limiting off-spring to 2 per couple, it is not logical to offer large deductions and tax allowances to more than 2 or 3 children per family. Tax relief in the short-run may be just and fair to help families who already have more than 2 children, but discussion must begin immediately to reverse that policy in the next ten or fifteen years.

There is a recommendation for an immediate Guaranteed Annual Income for all single-parent families, although in principle the Commission feels the G.A.I. should eventually be available for everyone.

The question of whether or not legal reforms are a valid interim step toward substantially improving the status of an unjustly treated group of people is a hard one to answer. It is a question which the movement for civil rights for Blacks in the United States is still debating. There is no doubt that the legal right to be hired, paid an equal wage and promoted on merit is a relief and benefit to those to whom those rights were denied, regardless of whether or not the underlying prejudices against those rights still exist. On the other hand, one gets the feeling that many recommendations for legal reforms in the Royal Commission Report would impose layer upon layer of bureaucracy and government control which citizens have less and less involvement in, and which, in addition to becoming top-heavy, absorb all the prejudices of society as have wads of water-soaked cotton-batting, and become — instead of reforms — instruments of the oppression already existing in society's attitudes. A current example of such "reforms" is the government employment offices, now called "Canada Manpower Centers". Originally intended to do something about unemployment by matching men and jobs, they have re-enforced the class injustice of our society by dealing with highly employable unemployed and have left to the departments of welfare the unskilled, the young, the unwed mother.

And so the Royal Commission's Information Centres to help all women will become receiving homes for the poor; day care centres will fall into the morass of the public school system and the Guaranteed Annual Income for one-parent families will become Welfare, with a big capital W.

But on the other hand not to make any legislative reforms at all while the real revolution — in consciousness-raising, changes in relationships between men and women, and the nature of work

216

and production — is taking place ...? That's a hard one! And I feel as trapped as the Commissioners may have. A number of areas, however, may be approached differently.

In establishing day care, the Commission recommends a network of Day Care Centres set up and run by governments (in cost sharing plans) which may eventually be part of the public education system. At a time when the public school system is being carefully and very critically examined, and being challenged by the establishment of privately run schools trying a variety of experiments — all to good — why add more children and more structure into that system? Denmark allows any 20 parents who have organised a private school at any level for their own children to apply to the government for subsidy to run their school. Why not begin moving in that direction in Canada with Day Care Centres? The obvious criticism to this suggestion is that the most depressed and needy families will not get themselves organised to establish the day care and apply for the subsidy. That will have to be the job of community organizers, women's lib activists and poor people's coalitions: a messier system on paper, but one which is consistent with the values of decentralization, community control, and parental involvement in education.

The question of class is a major dilemma in the current Women's Lib movement in North America: class differences among all women. Some Women's Lib groups like the Leila Kahlisl Collective in Toronto attempted to deal with this when they wrote that the primary institutional changes that must be brought about have to do with the ownership of property and production, wages and economic exploitation — in other words, our present capitalist system. Groups like the New Feminists in Toronto by-pass the class problem by saying that women share a common oppression vis-à-vis men that transcends differences in class interest and income.

The best example that explodes the analysis of the New Feminists is the question of servants, euphemistically known as "help in the home." It is not uncommon for a middle-class Women's Lib activist to hire a baby-sitter or a cleaning woman for a wage she herself would not work for. Nor is it uncommon to hear a woman talk about wanting to get out of the house and get a job in order to be creative, and then in the next breath say it doesn't "pay" to go to work because "you have to pay so much for help." Until a woman who goes to work is prepared to pay everything she earns, minus her expenses to the woman with whom she trades jobs, she is exploiting her both psychologically and economically as much as any man does. One can argue that within our present system simply trading jobs is not practical. Correctly so! But in saying that, one is admitting that our present system is the primary source of exploitation and must be changed. In other words, if we paid for cars, land, pharmaceuticals, medical care, heating oil, and packaged food an amount that gave a modest income to those who derive profit from those things, we could afford to pay a far higher proportion of our income for direct services.

The Royal Commission Report does not recognize this dilemma, and argues out of both sides of the mouth, especially in the chapter on "Women in the Family." The recommendations in the chapter on "Women in the Economy" assume the validity of our present system of paying income and wages, and aim to force equal payment for men and women. The recommendations in the chapter on taxation assume that people go to work primarily to make more money (which they do and have to, under our present system) and aim to change the tax laws so that working mothers can keep more of their wage.

A further contradiction comes in the chapter on the family when the Commission finds itself defending both the mother who wants to go to work, hire someone to do her house and child-care work, and bring additional income into the house; and the woman who tries to make a living, often supporting her own family doing house and childcare work, and who needs a decent income. The Commission is also against poverty which the Dominion Bureau of Statistics defined as $4,060 or less for a family of four. Since the average cleaning woman in Montreal, often a woman alone with three children, gets $10 to $12 a day, her annual income is well below the poverty line (and no paid holidays either). Sixteen dollars a day would put her at the poverty line, yet this is a wage which hardly any middle-class woman pays a cleaning woman. Many families could easily pay this kind of wage but *don't*. Others who would hire, not a cleaning woman perhaps, but a child-care worker so the mother can work, *cannot* pay this wage which would amount to a third or a half of the family income.

Obviously the nuclear family is a trap for women or families who want to expand their choices, but genuinely do not want to exploit another woman in the process.

What about communal arrangements? Many, many young people, Women's Liberation activists or not, are exploring alternatives to the nuclear family. There are many reasons for this movement, but basically the advantages are the economy of owning things in common, including spacious living quarters, the freedom resulting from shared chores, and the sociability of more than two adults. Clearly the result of four adults (two couples, for example) equally sharing housework gives each one individually the freedom that would accrue from hiring a cleaning woman at an exploitive wage. An alternative would be four adults working full-time outside the home paying the entire salary of one of them to a full-time housekeeper. There could be various combinations of these two alternatives.

Communal arrangements can also have the advantage of more than two children (remember: we're concerned with population growth) growing up together. There are many other advantages discussed amply in the Women's Lib literature.

Another area where class differences clash in a major way is that of co-operatively run day care, and the standards and values it will maintain. The Royal Commission by-passes this whole issue by advocating state-run centres which will result in an unimaginative school system with some differences in educational philosophy depending on the residential area, but basically inflexible.

Regarding day care, middle-class parents are usually clear and firm about their standards for light, space and numbers, and are willing to pay for them as much as they can. Poor parents would be too, if they had the money, and if they had the same standards in their homes; but it is unbalanced to pay for the one or two youngest children to have the light and space that the rest of the family cannot afford to have at home, and a family can easily feel resentful (and it does) that the State is willing to pay for the little children to have surroundings away from their home that it will not contribute toward helping the whole family have in their home. No amount of head-start, day care, home help or choices for women will make much difference in freeing people — women and all — as long as our society maintains a wage system which pays for essential services we all want and need like cleaning, loading, delivering, pressing, with a wage that cannot allow families to live decently.

Co-operative day care — with the best will in the world between neighbors like a mixed-class neighbourhood (like the Milton-Parc area in Montreal) — will heighten this clash. Not only is agreement on physical standards a problem, agreement on behavioural standards is more of a problem, and again with good economic and social reasons. Three-year-olds of middle class parents with the prospect of schooling that may encourage creative thinking, a room of their own with space for their 'doings', and best of all, a job which allows and encourages creative scope (and if it doesn't, it should! Speak to the new crop of law, medical, teaching and social work students!) will gain from day care that allows children to toilet-train themselves, put all the furniture in the middle of the room, and splash paint and water. Not so the three-year-old who must be ready for the rigidity of the ghetto-forty-in-a-classroom school by age 6, be ready to deliver groceries for long hours after school or baby-sit in the suburbs by age 12, and work for an employer who is not the least interested in hearing his or her creative opinion much less acting on it. That three-year-old must learn very early to 'behave', and nothing fills the parents with more fear and anguish than the thought that their son won't be able to get and hold a job, or their daughter marry a man who will do so. The most obvious indication that it is the fear of being without a job and of starving that alone has created the rigidity of working class child-rearing is that the present generation of all classes no longer in danger of starving, has often rejected those standards and simply refuses to work.

When there may no longer be a danger of starving, parents still hold old standards; besides, they still want new comforts, and as long as they must work obediently and with their mouths shut, they cannot, afford to support schooling — at any level — that will give their off-spring 'fancy ideas'. And as long as our society pays low wages, produces not for human need but for profit, and maintains a balast of unemployed to keep everyone on his toes, those values will be essential to the survival of the working class and proletariat.

The Royal Commission Report is genuinely concerned with finding ways within the framework of "liberal democratic" reform of allowing women scope and choice in their lives beyond their traditional role of raising children and keeping house. But as long as millions of people — male and female — must work so they can barely survive, while others reap the surplus, to speak of choices without major economic institutional change is not nearly enough.

The above essay is reprinted from *Our Generation*, vol. 8, No. 2, April 1972.

WHY WE NEED A WOMEN'S BUREAU
IN QUEBEC

by

Caroline Pestieau

The Royal Commission Report just confirmed what we knew by experience — that women in Canada are unable to exercise their full rights as citizens and are very often prevented both from fulfilling themselves as people and from contributing to society as they would wish to do. Voluntary associations, individuals, and corporations, who were convinced by the Report's arguments, can do a lot to redress the inferior status of women in Canada. But improvement, if it is left to private initiative, will come intolerably slowly. By now everyone knows that laissez-faire liberalism is not the answer to situations in which one class or group voluntarily or involuntarily exploits another. Government must take action: outlawing discrimination within its ranks and promoting the interests of the disadvantaged group.

Quebec is one of two Canadian provinces to have no Bureau, Office, or other public agency to promote the interests of women. Nor is there any legislation here against unequal pay and discriminatory hiring based on sex. (The 1964 law against discrimination in employment is a farce: maximum fine $100, no mention of marital status, no protection against reprisals by the employer. Some members of the Department of Labour think it is *ultra vires* anyway.) The need for a Women's Bureau is just as great in Quebec as elsewhere, perhaps even greater.

To start with, Quebec women need readily accessible information on a very wide range of subjects — legal, medical, financial, and educational. They need to know what is offered by the numerous service groups working in both languages. These groups themselves need to know where they can usefully expand their activities without futile confrontation with provincial government projects. A well-funded private organization could acquire and pass on information, but the necessity for frequent consultation with government departments and the need to coordinate activities in many different communities make us think that a public body would do the job better.

Information is not all. As we gather it, it becomes obvious that legal reform is overdue in many fields closely concerning women and that public policies are often ill-adapted to the needs of half the population. But lack of data justifies public and corporate apathy. How many women are not receiving alimony or child support because there is no machinery for following up defaulting husbands? How many women who laboriously completed night school vocational courses found that these were dead-end credits and had to take the nearest unskilled job? How many isolated housewives (fully trained at the taxpayers' expense) are receiving psychiatric care? No one knows. Until someone has the means and the time to find out, it will be difficult to get government and industry to undertake real changes.

And even if the National Assembly passed legislation outlawing sex discrimination in the labor market, as the Ontario Government did in 1970, it would be useless without follow-up machinery. Private citizens could refer flagrant cases to the relevant tribunal, but, in most instances, plaintiffs would need help in preparing their case and full assurances against reprisals by employers. In the absence of complaints, spot-checking would often reveal that female employees with seniority have not been offered the further training or promotion accorded to more recently hired male employees. Only an official body would have the authority and the continuity to carry out such spot-checks across the labour market.

Just correcting abuses is still an insufficient answer to the problem. We must not be caught administering Law XYZ and arguing over job descriptions while the whole structure of society, and of its traditional cell — the family — is changing out of recognition. Research and development on the future role of women requires resources. It also needs to be done in dialogue with the other planning agencies in the province, which are increasingly to be found in government departments. A Womens' Bureau at government level would look at public policy, present and proposed, from the point of view of women — something that has not yet been done. It would draw attention to negative consequences, for women, of policies that are usually only looked at from a narrowly departmental angle. More important, it would help orientate government thinking at the policy-making level

222

so that it may respond to the real needs of the neglected half of the population.

Such a Bureau, responsible for all the tasks mentioned above and many others, would be an entirely new institution. It would have to be attached to the highest level of provincial government — the prime minister's office — to assure it access and authority in case of interdepartmental jealousies. It would take the initiative in coordinating services to women, in rooting out discrimination, and in proposing long term policies in the interests of women. The Bureau would have to be particularly attentive to its constituents — Quebec women. Mechanisms to insure this, such as obligatory public auditions to discuss the annual report of activities and the collaboration of women chosen by the constituents, should be written into its constitution. Finally *the bureau would be temporary*. It is an anomaly in society that requires the creation of a Women's Bureau. Once the anomaly has disappeared the bureau will be dissolved. This must be laid down in the bill establishing it.

In December, 1971, the Fédération des Femmes du Québec addressed a brief to M. Bourassa requesting the creation of a Women's Bureau with the power to carry out the tasks described here. The brief was favorably received and the Prime Minister set up a joint committee (civil servants and representatives of the FFQ) to study the question. The committee presented its report at the beginning of the summer 1972 ...

CRITIQUE OF THE FEMINIST MOVEMENT

IDEOLOGY, CLASS, AND LIBERATION
by
Marlene Dixon

In the early growth stages of any protest movement unity is an overriding necessity. This was particularly true of the women's movement, since the status of women had deteriorated so markedly since the 1930's (and anti-woman propaganda had so discredited earlier women's movements) that there existed almost no widespread recognition that discrimination against women was a social evil. As far as the dominant culture was concerned, discrimination against women was a positive good, sanctioned by God and biology. Thus, the second upsurge of women's protest since the decline of the suffrage movement began with only a tiny band of activists and militants whose early demands for equality were met with ridicule from the powers and greeted with fearful denials and a sense of personal threat by the vast majority of women. The ideology of the new movement was primarily dictated by the necessities of early organizing, and those necessities were, above all, to gain legitimacy and recruits, which required, above all, unity.

As a consequence of the need for unity there developed a public ideology based upon feminism, opposition to discrimination and sisterhood. Obviously, what all women did understand was daily life at home or on the job (i.e., personal troubles) and the evils of discrimination.

On the other hand, antagonizing liberals was held by many to be an unwise strategy. It was felt that recognition of the legitimacy of women's demands for equality was dependant upon wrenching support out of the male liberal establishment. This was particularly true of those women who greatly feared being publicly contaminated by too close a connection with "bra-burning" left-leaning Women's Liberation.

All of these factors taken together mean that the women's movement recruited new members and struggled to gain public recognition on the basis of its liberal, public ideology — that peculiar amalgamation of feminism, discrimination as immoral and the mystique of sisterhood. It is to this public ideology and its class character that we shall now turn.

I: Sisterhood

The stress of the early and primitive ideology of Women's Liberation was on psychological oppression and social and occupational discrimination. The politics of psychological oppression and invoking the injustice of discrimination were aimed at altering the consciousness of women newly recruited to the movement in order to transform personal discontent into political militancy. Women, being in most cases without a political vocabulary, can more easily respond to the articulation of emotions (this, of course, explains the impassioned, personal nature of the polemical literature.) Furthermore, women of almost any political persuasion or lack of one can easily adopt the straightforward demand for social equality. Explaining the necessity for the abolition of social classes, the complexities of capitalism and its necessary evolution into imperialism, and the like, is a much more formidable task, often eliciting more hostility than sympathy.

The stress on discrimination aims directly at the liberal core of Canadian politics. In turn, sex discrimination affects all women, irrespective of race, language or class (but that it does not affect all women in the same way or to the same degree is often absent from discussion!) Furthermore, the demand for equality is a socially legitimate protest demand (whereas advocating social revolution is not!) The result of the primacy of ideologies of oppression and discrimination (and the absence of ideologies condemning exploitation) is to facilitate the recruitment of large numbers of women almost exclusively from the middle class.

The politics of oppression and the politics of discrimination are amalgamated and popularized in the ethic of sisterhood. Sisterhood invokes the common oppression of all women, the common discrimination suffered by all. Sisterhood is the bond, the strength, the glory of the women's movement; it is the call to unity, based on the idea that common oppression creates common understanding and common interests upon which all women can unite (transcending class, language and race lines) to bring about a vast movement for social justice — after first abolishing the special
228

privileges enjoyed by all men naturally. Sisterhood is a moral imperative: disagreements are to be minimized, no woman is to be excluded from the movement, all sisters are to love all other sisters, all sisters are to support all sisters: a veritable orgy of sisterly communion.[1]

The ethic of sisterhood does operate very powerfully to assure unity in the movement, e.g., the proscription against public attacks against any women; the outward united front position of Women's Liberation; keeping the ideological struggle internal to the movement. Sisterhood, and the sentiments of unity it fosters, does help to protect the movement from acutely destructive sectarianism, and it certainly provides enormous psychological strength and support to women who are openly rebelling for the first time in their lives.

Yet the ethic of sisterhood also disguises and mystifies the internal class contradictions of the women's movement. Specifically, sisterhood temporarily disguises the fact that all women do *not* have the same interests, needs, desires: working class women and middle class women, student women and professional women, anglophone women and francophone women have more *conflicting* interests than could ever be overcome by their common experience based on sex discrimination. The illusions of sisterhood are possible because Women's Liberation is a middle class movement — the voices of poor and working class women are only infrequently heard, and anglophone and francophone voices are heard separately.

The collapse of sisterhood will not result from any broadening of the class base of the movement, which will remain middle and lower middle class. It will result from growing political divergence, particularly over the emergence of ideologies of feminism which are openly reactionary. Perhaps more importantly, it will collapse because women will presumably fail to create human relationships that differ from those of the society at large. Just as in a male dominated movement the men most skilled at verbal persuasion and personal aggressiveness are the 'powers', so among women the most skilled at emotional manipulation dominate the vast collection of cliques that make up the movement. Struggles for power are intrinsically oppressive, and they can become very ugly, and a lot of people get hurt.[2] Somewhere in that process, sisterhood will probably meet its death.

II: Feminism

The ideologies which may be termed 'feminist' are many and varied. For purposes of parsimony, only two versions, liberal and reactionary radical feminism, will be discussed. However, it is important to remember that there are at least three basic feminist tenets: (1) First priority must be placed upon the liberation (however 'liberation' is understood) of women; (2) action programs ought to put first priority upon woman-centered issues (this is sometimes also combined with a demand to boycott any actions which are not women-centered). The position is tactically incorrect because it isolates the women's movement; it is politically incorrect because it does not understand the inter-relationship between the oppression of women and imperialism[3]; (3) any revolution that does not entail the liberation of women is of no interest to women, or ought to be repudiated by women.[4]

Underlying the nominal agreement on basic tenets of Feminism, two contradictory lines of analysis were present from the inception of the movement. One line stems from the assertion that 'men are the enemy' and that the primary contradiction is between men and women. The second analysis argues that the system (and the 'system' could mean different things, e.g., internal class contradictions, imperialism, etc.) is the cause of the oppression of women, in which some men are the enemy but most men are dupes, bribed through their privileged position over women to divide the people's struggle (i.e., male chauvinism, like racism, is false class consciousness).

The first analysis has the merit of simplicity, since locating the enemy presents no problem; the second analysis has the merit of being correct, but the disadvantage of being complicated. At the moment, the ethic of sisterhood smoothes over these two opposing conceptions of the enemy, i.e., who and what is going to have to be abolished to accomplish the liberation of women.

One can immediately see that the second analysis, pointing to class and property relations as the source of the oppression of women is much more difficult to propagandize than the first. In everyday life what all women confront is the bullying exploitation of men, particularly if they are middle class and unmarried. From the job to the bedroom, men are the enemy. But men are not the same *kind* of enemy to all women.

For a middle class woman, particularly if she has a career or is planning to have a career, the primary problem is to get men out of the way, (i.e., freeing women from male dominance

230

maintained by institutionalized discrimination), in order to enjoy the full privileges of middle class status. It is the system of sexual inequality, and not class exploitation, that is the primary source of middle class female protest. Given this fact, it is men, and not the very organization of the social system itself, who stand in the way. Consequently, it is reform of the existing system which is required, and not the abolition of existing property relations, not revolution — which would sweep away the privileges of middle class status.

The fact that the fight against discrimination is essentially a liberal reform program is mystified by the assertion that the equalization of the status of women would bring about a 'revolution' because it would alter the structure of the family and transform human relationships (which are held to be perverted through the existence of male authoritarianism). However, equalization of the status of women is not, nor will be, the cause of the decomposition of the nuclear family, obviously. The organization of the family is a result of the existing economic structure. Furthermore, equalization of the status of women is no more likely to introduce an era of beautiful human relationships than did the introduction of Christianity bring obedience to the Golden Rule or the Ten Commandments. The claim that status equalization would bring about 'revolution' is of the same order as the claim made by the Suffragists that giving women the vote would usher in an era of world peace.[5] Ideologically, the claims for the revolutionary results of the equalization of the status of women is a compromise worked out between the liberals and the radicals within the movement, i.e., enabling the liberals to co-opt the revolutionary rhetoric of the left.

Liberal Feminists do not openly admit that their ideology is a variant on 'men are the enemy.' Instead they adopt the forgiving, materialistic view that men are 'misguided' and that through education and persuasion (legal if need be) can be brought around to accepting the equalization of the status of women. Since the question of the origins of injustice and the roots of social power are never very strong elements in any liberal ideology, there is little besides legislative reforms and education to fall back on.[6]

The brand of Feminism based upon the assertion that 'men are the principal enemy' in turn branches into liberal Feminism and what may be termed "radical reactionary Feminism". Reactionary Feminism takes as its fundamental tenet that *all men are the enemies of all women,* and in its most extreme form, calls for the subjugation of all men (and sometimes for the extermination

231

of all men). If we were to construct the vision of the future society (presumably what the revolution would create) it seems clear that it is not only wanting in certain humanitarian feelings, but raises a very nasty spectre. One grants that such an Utopia would be revolutionary, but one shudders to compute the portion of the gross national product that would have to be set aside to maintain the Female R.C.M.P., the Female Provincial Police (Pink Coats?) and the manufacture and maintenance of the requisite concentration camps for Male State Criminals and Political Offenders. Even a 'final solution to the male question' presents numerous logistical problems (after all, half of the world's population makes an awfully large heap of ashes). Of course, one could try the South African solution, but this is somewhat discouraging, as some people do have a tendency to rebel while others have a tendency to fraternize, and so the system would most likely be plagued by considerable instability.

Of course, reactionary radical feminism does not outline its Utopia, in fact, it rarely follows the logical outcome of the position to its conclusion (although in many cases it might not make much difference). Reactionary feminism is not an ideology of revolution, (the likelihood of victory seeming remote even to its advocates), but an ideology of vengeance. It is also a profound statement of despair, which sees the cruelty and ugliness of present relationships between men and women as immutable, inescapable.[7]

Reactionary feminism may be politically confused, but it powerfully expresses the experience and feeling of a whole segment of the female population. Reactionary feminism has found its greatest stronghold in the city of New York, the cruellest city, no less for women than for others. Yet the phenomenon is found in all large North American cities. Masses of women, born into the middle class, often well educated, flood the offices employed as clerks, telephone operators, low level editors, typists, secretaries. They are poorly paid, their jobs are not respected, they have little job security. The humiliations heaped upon their heads at work are nothing to what happens in the sexual marketplace, where competition for men is ferocious, and where the men exploit the situation to the fullest. Many novels, films and plays have depicted this world. Alas, the authors were primarily men, and little suspected the feelings of hatred and bitterness that women disguised so well. The quintessence of that hatred and bitterness was the genius of Valerie Solanis; it is also reflected in a well known cartoon in which a lovely woman contemplates a heap of human bones with an expression of sublime satisfaction. The

232

caption reads: "He asked her to eat him and she did."

The root of reactionary feminism is in the sexual exploitation of women, and finds its stronghold amongst unmarried middle class women in the large cities. Its strength lies in the fact that it does express and appeal to psychological oppression, for this oppression is far worse than the conditions of economic exploitation experienced by these women.

The great weakness of all left wing ideologies in women's liberation (as a middle class movement) is that they never adequately understand or speak to the realities of sexual exploitation. Even uncompromising leftist women will sit to one side while a reactionary feminist has the floor with a soft smile and narrowed eyes, for the anger runs deep and the wounds are daily re-opened. Furthermore, the mechanical repetition of "socialism first and then women's liberation" or the even more idiotic claim that socialism by itself would accomplish the liberation of women, is so patently false, so remote from the inner turmoil experienced by women, that it discredits all the more left wing analysis.

The fact is that socialism will *not* guarantee the liberation of women and the U.S.S.R. is an example of the simple fact. Socialism without question improves the material conditions of women, and creates new opportunities, but one might argue that the same can as easily be accomplished under capitalism. The inability or unwillingness to talk about communist society, the social revolution which must be built on the foundation of economic revolution, only lead to the rejection of a 'socialist' utopia, and leave the way clear for the spread of reactionary ideologies. In the last analysis reactionary feminism is a product of male supremacy and sexual exploitation. Male dominance, itself reactionary, breeds reaction.

As a final note, it should be understood that reactionary feminism is also a middle and lower middle class phenomenon. For working class and especially poor women, even though the expression of male chauvinism is more exploitative and often far more brutal, it is also much easier to see the ways in which men are oppressed. Women are able to understand the sources of the aimless violence, they know at first hand the ravages of unemployment and enforced pauperization that create the psychological despair which is a class component of male chauvinism. For many poor and working class women, no matter how much they are prepared to improve life for themselves and for their children including struggling against male chauvinism in their own men, the anti-male line is repugnant and keeps many of these women from being able to relate at all to Women's Liberation. Furthermore, the daily experience with acute exploitation makes it very clear that it is not men who are the enemy, but the wealthy who are the enemy.[8]

A final variant on feminism is the assertion that 'women will make the revolution.' Women will make the revolution can mean two quite different things: one is, quite literally, that women will make the revolution because men are too corrupt, too self-interested and too bound up with the oppression of people, especially females, to *ever* be trusted as allies. This position stems from conceptualizing men as the primary enemy.

The second position involves a two-stage argument: (1) there exists a contradiction between men and women based upon a monopoly of social power in the hands of men, thus the first step is to create a power base for women which will equalize the power relationships between men and women; (2) men and women will then be able to relate to each other from the base of their own power (represented for women by an autonomous women's movement) permitting an equal partnership (in the form of alliances and coalitions) in class struggle. The internal contradictions may thus be resolved and class struggle undertaken (however, the steps are not seen as discrete, one following the other, but evolving dialectically through organization and practice).

The problem with the notion that *only* women will make the revolution is that it overlooks what it most often points out: women are half, only half, of the population. If it isn't likely that the men are going to do it alone, neither are the women. Furthermore, all women are *not* going to make the revolution: lady psychologists are not going to return to the factory; rich women are not going to give up their elegant houses to go on welfare and the middle class housewife is not going to become a professional revolutionary.

The whole ideology of 'women alone are going to make the revolution' is cloaked in mysticism, invoking an ill-defined vision of *Women's* exotic powers that can somehow bring about the just society in a way totally different from your common, garden variety 'male dominated' revolution, e.g., violence is *male,* therefore the women's revolution will not be violent, it will be, — what? (Hexing the ruling class has not as yet demonstrated that it can stop a bullet, discourage the police, shorten a prison sentence or overthrow the system). The mysticism of "special powers" is much more gratifying than a dismal theory which does not

234

see the superiority of women, but which describes a painfully unglamorous process requiring objective social and economic conditions, hard work, total commitment, hard thinking (which is in any case 'elitist') effective organizing, the capacity to seize power and a lot of luck — in which bleeding every twenty-eight days is simply not sufficient to pull it off.

The meaning of 'women will make the revolution' lies in the fact that it articulates the position of women who have decided that the realities of male chauvinism make it absolutely necessary to create an autonomous women's movement. The decision to form a separate and autonomous movement is a direct result of understanding the roots of male chauvinism, i.e., that the basis of the unequal relationship between men and women is power, not attitudes.

An autonomous movement would create power where little has existed before, create a new consciousness of the subjugation of women, and raise profound issues about the nature and organization of the left movement.

As this essay attempts to outline, many forces were at work to drive left radical women into a relatively isolated position within Women's Liberation. From a position of relative weakness, these women are often helpless to stem the tide of either liberalism or reaction. Again, it is so clearly a case of reactionary male chauvinism creating a reactionary women's movement. The lessons from 'women will make the revolution' are clear: the basis of the oppression of women is power, and the resolution of the contradiction is not a matter of moral persuasion or individual therapy. Male privilege is not given up voluntarily, it must be taken away. Overall the whole saga of Women's Liberation testifies most clearly to a very paramount truth: a progressive revolutionary movement cannot contain within itself the contradictions of oppression, inequality and special privilege.

III: Conclusion

Women's Liberation focuses almost exclusively upon psychological oppression and sexual exploitation. This can be explained by the fact that Women's Liberation was first a student, and then a student-age movement. The youthful constituency of Women's Liberation faces different problems than those of older, married and largely professional women. Furthermore, the revulsion with liberal politics which is characteristic of modern student movements is also typical of Women's Liberation.

235

The programs actually undertaken by Women's Liberation reflect the overriding problems of younger women: the need for legal abortion since many unmarried girls are oppressed by unwanted pregnancies and the brutal experience of obtaining an illegal abortion); the demand for day care centers by those young women who do have children, but whose husbands — just starting out in their careers — cannot provide the resources which would free a restless young wife from the drudgery of constant child care; the creation of women's centers and small group meetings, to provide young women with a 'place of their own' in which to socialize, to work for abortion on demand, the day care center or help women in distress. As young, unmarried non-student women are beginning to be recruited to the movement, agitation at the workplace (office, telephone company, etc.) is beginning in a very modest way around modest issues (not being forced to wait on the boss with coffee, obtaining the right to dress as one pleases, or better pay and hours). Prison experience on the part of young politicals has begun to raise the issues of women prisoners — establishing one of the first real links with Quebec and poor women. The rise of gay liberation and the open participation of lesbians in Women's Liberation also brings the major source of working and lower class influence to the movement, since the gay community, equally suffering universal legal and social persecution, tends to be a very mixed and egalitarian society. Nonetheless, the major issues and the major concerns remain predominantly reflective of the life-styles and needs of unmarried, youthful, middle and lower middle class girls.

An emphasis upon economic exploitation (rather than psychological oppression and sexual exploitation) which could have begun to reveal the internal class contradictions within the women's movement is almost totally absent from the ideological mainstream of Women's Liberation. However, it is in no way surprising that such would be the case. Women's politics are dominated by problems of psychological oppression since the major oppression experienced by middle class women is not material, but psychological.

Given the almost exclusive attention to sexual exploitation and the consequent psychological oppression, the result is to focus not upon male supremacy, but upon its result, the practice of male chauvinism; not upon the need for revolutionary social and economic changes, but upon individualized struggles between men and women around the oppressive attitudes and objective sexual and social privileges of men. Furthermore, emphasis upon male chauvinism has the effect of privatizing the contradiction between men and women, transmuting the conflict into problems of personal relationships, rather than politicizing the conflict as part of the overall capitalist system of economic and class exploitation.

The result in the production of an ideology, unique to women's liberation, which focuses upon the individual relationship between men and women, and between women and women (cf. Schulamith Firestone's analysis). This ideology is an important component of reactionary radical Feminism, it is powerfully related to the widespread adoption of lesbian relationships as a means of escaping the male-female relationship, and it is also the ideological basis for the small group. (In the small group women are to seek each other out for emotional support and in helping one another to understand the full extent of the oppression contained within male-female relationships.)

Politics are almost completely non-existent in the small group which is essentially a source of social and psychological support. It is quite possible that for the majority of women in Women's Liberation, membership in a small group is the full extent of participation. Rivalries, disputes and feuds often grow up between small groups in the same city, frequently having the effect (along with major action and ideological divisions between present day Politicos and Feminists) of making even the minimal workings of a women's center impossible.

Nonetheless, the origin and key importance of the small group is to be found in the fundamental tenet of Women's Liberation: organize around your own oppression. There are many foundations for such a position. First, the major task faced by early organizers was to get women to admit that they in fact were feeling oppressed. The socialization of women includes a vast superstructure of rationalizations for women's secondary status; the superstructure of belief is reinforced through inducing guilt and fear (of not being a 'true women' etc.) as a response to rebellion against women's traditional role; finally, women are raised to be very conservative, to cling to the verities of the hearth, to a limited and unquestioning acceptance of things as they are. However, it was very quickly learned that under the crust of surface submission there had built up in countless women an enormous frustration, anger, bitterness — what Betty Friedan called "an illness without a name." Women's Liberation has given the illness a name, an explanation, and a cure. The cure is the small group, and the method is what the Chinese Communists call "Speaking Bitterness." The bitterness, once spoken, is almost overwhelming in its sheer emotional impact.

Originally, the aim of the small group was supposed to have been the path to sisterhood — that unity expressed in empathic identification with the suffering of all women — and from sisterhood to politics, and from politics to revolution.

However, the result of the class position of almost all recruits to Women's Liberation was to retranslate 'organize around your own oppression' to 'organize around your own interests.' The step from self-understanding to altruistic identification and cross class unity never occurred because the real basis for radicalization, objective economic exploitation and oppression, is absent.

Leftist women (particularly this one) made a great tactical blunder: seeing that women could only be organized in terms of their own subjective oppression; seeing the common oppression of all women (irrespective of class); aiming at radicalizing the constituency of Women's Liberation, we talked a great deal about the common source of oppression (hoping to foster the 'empathic identification' that would provide the bridge to cross class unity) but we talked much less about the fact that the common oppression of women *has different results in different social classes.*

What leftists have not taken into account is the fact that middle class women do not *want* to identify with their class inferiors; don't care, by and large, what happens to women who have problems different from their own; and greatly dislike being reminded that they are richer, better educated, healthier and have more life chances than most people. This whole attitude can be summed up in a comment made to me in Washington, D.C. by Jessie Bernard: "We have to take care of our own problems first" — she might well have added, first, last and always.

Organize around your own oppression is indeed a Pandora's Box of troubles. Middle class women use this maxim to justify their own class interests: we are oppressed too. Middle class women use the maxim to justify ignoring the mass of lower and working class women: 'ending our oppression will end theirs, i.e., the fight against discrimination would equalize the status of all women. Worst of all, middle class women defend their own position by replying to possible criticism "we are not only also oppressed, we are equally oppressed."

In sum, the numerous cases where the small group changes from its original consciousness raising function into a mechanism for social control and group therapy is a result of the predominantly

238

middle class character of Women's Liberation. The fact that there are so few women who are directly experiencing material deprivation, poverty, threats of genocide or enforced pauperization — that is, are not driven by conditions of objective exploitation and deep social oppression, makes it almost inevitable that the search for cultural and life-style changes is substituted for radical and revolutionary politics. The relative wealth and privilege of middle class people makes it possible for them to envision a good life within the system as it is, even to create such a life through counter-culture forms such as communal living, or adopting lesbianism as a way to simply short circuit male sexual exploitation.

It all becomes painfully clear. From the self-interested position of a middle class women, Viet Nam can be written off as 'penis' war which women (who will never be soldiers) should ignore in order to press for liberation on the sexual front; imperialism is a wicked trick on the part of male chauvinist domineering elites and their female dupes whom women should ignore while fighting for day care for students and faculty; or while forging ahead with the abortion protests at the legislature; the exploitation of working class man and working class women is little more than commie cant (everyone *knows* in any case that the working class is ignorant and fascist, since the enlightened, liberal, kindly bourgeois Sociologists have confirmed this on numerous occasions).

In short, Women's Liberation, for all its rhetoric and all its pretensions, and for all of its brave start, has outwardly become what it really is (indeed, what it had to be): a reactionary middle class reform movement. Nonetheless, the movement has accomplished much, and much of what it has accomplished is not simply middle class reform. Women have won recognition for the justice of their cause; any left wing movement must beware to become demystified, revealed as a shoddy copy of the alienated and anti-human competitive careerism of the bourgeois world; the broad outlines of the liberating ideas of Women's Liberation are slowly spreading to third world groups and filtering into the working class; thousands of women have a chance now for a better life; large numbers of women have been politically mobilized who were before passive and conservative.

And finally, the women's struggle remains, the drive and the thirst for a decent society and a good life. So long as the woman's struggle remains, women remain a part of it, from birth to the grave.

1. If all this sounds ironically bitter, that's because it is, largely self-directed, i.e., my own one-time belief that women could transcend class language and race lines to form a single, radical movement. The psychological roots of these goings-on are related to the joy of being liberated from self-contempt, and a sense of belonging somewhere, at last!, in one's own right. The political roots are in the ostracism and general ugliness that one can suffer from a male dominated left.

2. The whole question of the internal structure of the movement is urgent, but it is also difficult and complicated. Above all what is needed is a critique of the "anti-elitist" ideology and its manipulation in the struggle for power. Such a discussion is unfortunately beyond the scope of this essay.

3. The basis for the refusal to join forces is a rejection of male opportunism, the desire of men to use women to fight their battles for them. It is the old familiar story of reactionary male chauvinism fostering reactionary feminism.

4. Conscious and unconscious anti-communism is greatly fostered by the latter point, as it is often argued that since women in Russia, Cuba, Viet Nam and China are not 'liberated' then socialism and communism ought to be rejected by women. Lack of any adequate knowledge of these revolutions makes such arguments sound convincing, even though the allegation is false. c.f., Jack Beldon, *China Shakes the World,* Wilfred Burchett, *Viet Nam North,* etc. On the loss of an entire generation of men (20 millions) in WW II and its effect on the status of women in Russia, see, Isaac Deutscher, *Stalin, a Political Biography.*

5. The belief that women were superior to men, that they were equipped with greater empathy, lovingness, and virtue (an ideology also held by the Suffragists) was widely accepted by women. For middle class women it is far from the truth. Social hypocricy, gossip, slander, emotional manipulation, envy, jealousy, disloyalty, extreme individualism (especially in competition for men) are the necessary results of a socially powerless and dependant position. Women's liberation is seeking, through the small group, to change some of these traits in women, but as the ideology of the "emotional and ethical superiority" of women spreads, it is no longer necessary to carry through the difficult process of self-changing. Women's behavior is never even included in codes of behavior which require some honor and honesty in conduct, since women are *expected* to be petty, spiteful and dishonest. Women, celebrating themselves, refuse to confront these results of a secondary status in their own behavior. The result is that the women's movement is often times more of a hell than the old male dominated movement used to be.

6. The discussion of social class and the question of discrimination and legislative reform should not lead one to reject legislative reform. Such reforms as would limit the current abuses of working women are real gains, and worth fighting for. The challenge is to make it crystal clear that legislative reforms are a very minor element in necessary changes, that work to the greater advantage of middle class people. It is possible to support efforts for legislative change, but only if a left set of demands (reflecting class interests) are not submerged and lost in the struggle. It is necessary, as the old socialists used to say, to be in the same march on occasion, but always under one's own banner.

7. Reactionary feminism requires a whole study in itself, so that only certain elements are treated here. For women who would like to pursue the interpretation that reactionary feminism as a species of fascism, at least ideologically,

consult Ernst Nolte, *Three Faces of Fascism* (Mentor, 1969). Note: when reading Nolte remember that his discussion is based, in some respects, on the Stalinist period in the U.S.S.R. Alternatives such as presented by Revolutionary China would lend a new corrective element to Nolte's thesis.

8. This characterization is true for poor white people, the author knows from experience. Furthermore, it is tiresome to have the reactionary politics of the most privileged sector of the working class, e.g., construction workers, always dredged up to show that the proletariat is fascist and the middle class enlightened. What I am trying to express is beautifully stated in the lovely and powerful film, *Salt of the Earth*. It is a great pity that the men who made that film were not able to put their understanding into practice, i.e., to make the liberation of women a basic leftist issue.

SELECTED BIBLIOGRAPHY

OF

CANADIAN PUBLICATIONS ON WOMEN

Allaire, Emilia. *Profils Féminins,* Garneau, Québec, 1967.

Anderson, William Ashley. *Angel of Hudson Bay: The True Story of Maud Watt,* Clarke, Irwin & Co., Toronto, 1961.

Bannermann, Jean. *Leading Ladies, 1639-1967,* Carrswood, Dundas, 1967.

Barrington, Gwenyth. *Women Without Money,* Longmans, Toronto, 1947.

Benston, Margaret, *The Political Economy of Women's Liberation,* Hogtown Press, Toronto, 1969.

Blackburn John H. *Land of Promise,* MacMillan of Canada, Toronto, 1970.

Canada, Department of Labour. *Women in the Public Service: Their Utilization and Employment,* by Stanislas Judek, Ottawa, 1968.

―――. *Maternity-Leave Policies. A Survey.* Ottawa, 1969.

―――. *Working Mothers and their Child-Care Arrangements,* Ottawa, 1970.

―――. Women's Bureau. *Women in the Labour Force 1970: Facts and Figures,* Ottawa, 1971.

Canada, Department of National Health and Welfare. *The Canadian Mother and Child,* Ottawa, 1967.

Canada. DBS, Special Labour Force Studies. *Women Who Work,* by John D. Allingham and Byron G. Spencer, Ottawa, 1967, 1968.

Canada, Public Service Commission. *Sex and the Public Service,* by Kathleen Archibald, Ottawa, 1970.

Canada, Royal Commission on the Status of Women in Canada. *Report,* Ottawa, 1970.

―――. STUDIES FOR THE ROYAL COMMISSION ON THE STATUS OF WOMEN IN CANADA:

Bertrand, Marie-Andrée. *Women in the Criminal Law.*

Bossen, Marianne. *Patterns of Manpower Utilization in Canadian*

Department Stores.

Bossen, Marianne. *Manpower Utilization in Canadian Chartered Banks.*

Bruce, Jean. *Eskimo Women in the Keewatin Region.*

Canadian Association of University Teachers. *A Comparison of Men's and Women's Salaries and Employment Fringe Benefits in the Academic Profession.* A study directed by Dr. R. A. H. Robson, with the assistance of Mireille Lapointe.

Canadian Welfare Council. *A Study of Family Desertion in Canada.*

Carisse, Colette, *Portrayal of Women by the Mass Media.*

Carver, Anne. *The Participation of Women in Political Activities in Canada.*

Clifford, Howard. *Day Care: An Investment in People.*

Eaton, Keith E. *Immigration and Citizenship Legislation Affecting Women in Canada.*

Ferguson, Edith. *Immigrant Women in Canada.*

Gaudet, Bérengère. *Study on Family Law.*

Geoffroy, Renée and Paule Sainte-Marie. *Attitudes of Union Workers to Women in Industry.*

Gwyn, Sandra. *Canadian Women and the Arts.* Based on essays by John Kraglund, Elizabeth Kilbourn, Nathan Cohen, J. Rudel-Tessier, Frank Daley, Alain Pontaut, Emmett O'Grady and Gilles Marcotte. Preface by Jean LeMoyne.

Hartle, Douglas G. *Taxation of the Incomes of Married Women.*

Hawkins, Freda. *Women Immigrants in Canada.*

Hobart, Charles W. *Changing Orientations to Marriage: A Study of Young Canadians.*

Hickling-Johnson Ltd. *The Present Role of Women in the Canadian Labour Force.*

Hickling-Johnson Ltd. *The Status of Women in the Field of Collective Bargaining.*

Johnson, Micheline D. *History of the Status of Women in the Province of Quebec.*

Labarge, Margaret Wade. *Cultural Tradition of Canadian Women: The Historical Background.*

Lacasse, François D. *Women at Home: The Cost to the Canadian Economy of the Withdrawal from the Labour Force of a Major Proportion of the Female Population.*

Lambert, Ronald D. *Sex-Role Imagery in Children: Social Origins of Mind.*

Lotz, Jim. *The Changing Role of Canadian Indian Women.*

MacLellan, Margaret E. *A History of Women's Rights in Canada.*

Parizeau, Alice. *Day-Care Services and Pre-School Education in Selected Countries.*

Porter, Arthur, *The Introduction and Impact of Technological Changes on Female Occupations: A Prospective Analysis.*

Quebec Federation of Women. *Participation of Women in Politics in Quebec.* A Study directed by Francine Départie.

Rotec Inc. *Projected Market Conditions for Female Labour in 1980.* An econometric analysis directed by André Larochelle.

Shipley, Nan. *The Status of the Indian and Métis Women of Manitoba.*

Silicoff, Joël A. *Labour Legislation Affecting Women in Canada.*

Silicoff, Joël A. *Credit Facilities for Women.*

Stirling, Robert M. *Effects of Wife's Employment on Family Relations.* A review of literature.

Thibeault, André. *Absenteeism and Turnover in the Female Labour Force.* A review of literature.

Canada Suffrage Association. *Report,* 1912.

Canadian Association for Adult Education. *What's in It?* (Summary of the *Report* of the Royal Commission on the Status of Women in Canada), Citizenship Branch, Department of Secretary of State, Ottawa, 1971.

CBC National Forum. *The Position of Women in Canada,* Dec. 11, 1938, Canadian Pamphlet Collection (No. 1004), change.

Canadian Council on Social Development. *Day Care. Report of a National Study,* Ottawa, 1972.

———. *The One Parent Family, Report of an Inquiry,* Ottawa, 1971.

Canadian Women's Educational Press. *Women Unite,* Toronto, 1972.

——. *The Day Care Book,* Toronto, 1972.

Casgrain, Thérèse, *Une Femme Chez les Hommes,* Editions du Jour, Montreal, 1972.

Clarkson, Adrienne. *True to you in my Fashion,* New Press, Toronto, 1971.

Cleverdon, Catherine Lyle. *The Women Suffrage Movement in Canada,* University of Toronto Press, Toronto, 1950.

Cockburn, Patricia. *Women University Graduates in Continuing Education and Employment,* Canadian Federation of University Women, Toronto, 1967.

French, Doris and Stewart, Margaret. *Ask no Quarter,* Longmans Green, Toronto, 1959.

Foster Anna. *The Mohawk Princess: Being some Account of the Life of Tekahion Wake (E. Pauline Johnson),* Lion's Gate Publishing Co., Vancouver, 1931.

Glass, Robert and Kase, Nathan. *Woman's Choice. A Guide to Contraception Fertility, Abortion and the Menopause,* Signet Books, Winnipeg, 1970.

Grain Grower's Guide, 1909-1916.

Gray, James H. *Red Lights on the Prairies,* MacMillan of Canada, Toronto, 1970.

Healy, William J. *Women of Red River,* Peguis Publishers, Winnipeg, 1967.

Haig, Kennethe M. *Brave Harvest: The Life Story of E. Cora Hind LL.D.,* 19xx.

Hobbs, Lisa. *Love and Liberation: Up Front with the Feminists,* 1972.

Innis, Mary Quayle. *The Clear Spitir*, University of Toronto Press, Toronto, 1967.

Kieran, Sheila. *The Non-Deductable Woman: A Handbook for Working Wives and Mothers*. MacMillan, Toronto, 1970.

LaMarsh, Judy. *Memoirs of a Bird in a Gilded Cage*, McClelland and Stewart, Toronto, 1969.

Landry, Avrom. *Marxism and the Woman Question*, Progress Publishing, Toronto, 1943.

LeMoyne, Jean. *Convergences*, Ryerson, Toronto, 1966. (Originally published in French)

McClung, Nellie, *Clearing in the West: My Own Story*, Thomas Allen, Toronto, 1935.

———. *In Times Like These*, McLeod and Allen, Toronto, 1915; new edition with an introduction by Veronica Strong-Boag, University of Toronto Press, Toronto, 1972.

———. *The Stream Runs Fast: My Own Story*, Thomas Allen, Toronto, 1935.

McDonald, Flora. *Women's Suffrage in Canada*, Toronto, 1912.

McWilliams, Margaret. *Manitoba Milestones*, Toronto, 1928.

———. Et al. *Post-War Problems of Women*, King's Printer, Ottawa, 1943.

Martin, Claire. *In an Iron Glove*, Ryerson, Toronto, 1968. (Originally published in French, under the title *Dans un Gant de Fer)*

Madsen, Pamela. *Where We're At: The Case of Women as a Subordinate Group*, University of Lethbridge, Lethbridge, 1972.

Moodie, Susanna. *Roughing it in the Bush*, McClelland and Stewart, Toronto, 1962. (First published in 1852)

National Council of Women of Canada. *Women in Canada*, 1900.

Ostry, Sylvia, *The Female Worker in Canada*, DBS monograph, Ottawa, 1968.

Paradis, Suzanne. *Femme Fictive – Femme Réelle*, Garneau, Québec, 1966.

Pelrine, Eleanor Wright. *Abortion in Canada*, New Press, Toronto, 1971.

Record of Proceedings in the Privy Council, No. 121 of 1929, On Appeal from the Supreme Court of Canada: In the Matter of a Reference as to The Meaning of the Word "persons" in Section 24 of the British North America Act, 1867. (Available in the Public Archives of Canada, Ottawa).

Riddel, William R. *Woman Franchise in Quebec*, 1900.

Rowntree, Mickey and John. *More on the Political Economy of Women's Liberation*, Hogtown Press, Toronto, 1971.

Ryerson, Stanley B. *Unequal Union*, Progress Books, Toronto, 1968.

Sanders, Byrne Hope. *Emily Murphy, Crusader*, MacMillan, Toronto, 1945.

————. *Famous Women,* Clarke, Irwin & Co., Toronto, 1958.

Seeley, John R., Sim, R. Alexander and Loosley, Elizabeth W., *Crestwood Heights,* University of Toronto Press, Toronto, 1963.

Shaw, Rosa L. *Proud Heritage,* Ryerson Press, Toronto, 1957.

Sinclair, Sonja. *I Presume You Can Type,* CBC Publications, Toronto, 1969.

Stowe-Gullen, Augusta, *History of the Formation of the National Council of Women,* Toronto, 1931.

Tessier, Albert, *Canadiennes,* Fidès, Montreal, 1962.

Traill, Catherine Parr. *The Backwoods of Canada,* McClelland and Stewart, Toronto, 1966. (First published in 1836).

————. *The Canadian Settler's Guide,* McClelland and Stewart, Toronto, 1969. (First published in 1855).

Van Stolk, Mary. *Man and Woman,* McClelland and Stewart, Toronto, 1968.

Zuker, Marvin and Callwood, June. *Canadian Women and the Law,* Copp, Clark Publishing Co., Toronto, 1971.

NOTES ON THE CONTRIBUTORS:

Freda Bain, a native Montrealer, holds a B.F.A. from Rhode Island School of Design. She is a printmaker, teaches printmaking at Dawson College, and has two children.

Anuradha Bose was born in Calcutta and was brought up in the never-never land of Anglo-India where feminist ideas and feminist good sense are juxtaposed with chiffon minds and chiffon saris. She teaches English at the CEGEP Bois-de-Boulogne, in Montreal, where she has been living since 1968.

Margit Boronkay came to Canada at the age of three and has since lived in Ottawa, Boston and Montreal. She holds a B.A. (Fine Arts) from Boston College. At the present time, she is assistant to the registrar, at Loyola of Montreal.

Elspeth Buitenhuis was born in Ontario. She holds a Ph.D. from McGill University, has two children and teaches English and Canadian Literature at Loyola of Montreal. She has published several articles, as well as one book.

Dagmar de Venster came to Montreal when she was in her twenties, from her native British Columbia. She had worked as a secretary and is presently a home-maker. She is in her fifties now, and takes evening courses at Loyola. The name is fictitious.

Marlene Dixon holds a Ph.D. from U.C.L.A. She is an exile in Canada: she has been teaching sociology at McGill ever since she was notoriously fired from the University of Chicago. She lives on her farm in Quebec, 60 miles out of Montreal. She is one of the early organisers of the Women's Liberation Movement, both in the U.S. and in Canada.

Lise Fortier, M.D., F.R.C.S.(C), is a well-known Montreal gynaecologist, Director of the Family Planning Clinic at Notre Dame Hospital, Montreal.

Shirley Gardiner is from Northern Quebec. She came to Montreal in 1964. She is a student at Sir George Williams University, has one child and is the Executive Editor of the *Handbook on Birth Control.*

Christine Garside came to Montreal in 1965. A Canadian citizen, she holds a Ph.D. from Claremont Graduate School in California. She teaches philosophy at Sir George Williams University, has two children and is the author of several articles on women, as well as of one novel.

Margaret Gillett, is professor of Education at McGill and Editor of the *McGill Journal of Education.* Dr. Gillett is author of many papers in professional journals and of books such as *A History of Education: Thought and Practice* and *The Laurel and the Poppy.* She came to Montreal in 1966.

Kathy Gower was born in Ohio and came to Montreal in 1970. She studies Communication Arts at Loyola.

Lin Green was born in Halifax. She came to Montreal twenty years ago. She works part-time, as a secretary, and is a student at Sir George Williams University.

Sylvia Green came to Montreal at the moment of Expo '67 during which she worked as a music supervisor in the Children's Creative Centre. Born in Toronto, she decided to stay in Montreal and taught in the public school system. She founded, in 1972, an elementary Free School — l'Ecole au Bord du Lac — on the Montreal Lakeshore.

Janet Kask is a Canadian citizen of American origin. She has two daughters, is a free-lance writer. She has worked for the C.B.C., the Canadian Press, and the *Montreal Star.* She is a member of the Montreal Writers' Cooperative.
250

Lucia Kowaluk came to Montreal in 1959, from the U.S. She holds an M.A.S.W. from McGill University, has one child, and is one of the editors of *Our Generation*.

Sharron Lee Smith is originally from Ottawa but has been living in Montreal for several years. She has worked as an executive secretary and is now a student at Sir George Williams University. She is also a writer and has published a collection of poetry, *Roses are for Eating;* some of her poetry has been included in a number of anthologies.

Jean McIllwrick came to Montreal at the age of one, from England. She has worked as a secretary and is presently unemployed. She has one child and takes evening courses at Loyola.

Katherine McGillivray came to Canada at the age of nine, from Vienna, Austria. She has been living in Montreal since 1961. She has two sons and is a communications consultant.

Mary Melfi came to Montreal as a small child, in 1957. She was born in Italy. She studies English at Loyola and plans to become a writer. She does not intend to specialise in Women's Liberation.

Judith B. Moody came to Montreal in 1970, from the U.S. She is working towards her Ph.D. in Geo-Chemistry, at McGill University.

Cerise Morris came to Montreal in 1956, from her native Alberta. She holds an M.A.S.W. from McGill and is the director of the Women's Center of the Y.W.C.A., in Montreal.

Edith Murphy came to Montreal in 1939, from Budapest, Hungary. She has three children and two grandchildren, works in retailing and takes evening courses at Loyola.

Inge Packer came to Montreal in 1938, from Germany. She has one daughter and is a home-maker. She is also very active in Adult Education and is presently chairman of the Women's Institute of the Congregation Shaar Hashomayim, in Montreal.

Beatrice Pearson is a native Montrealer. She is a home-maker as well as a full-time day student at Loyola. She has three children.

Caroline Pestiau came to Montreal in 1963, from the U.K. She has four children, is a free-lance economist and former vice-president of the Fédération des Femmes du Québec.

Lilian Reinblatt is a Montreal lawyer and a native of this city, too. She holds both a B.A. and a B.Sc. from Sir George Williams University, as well as a B.C.L. from McGill University. She has one daughter.

Mary Riopel has lived in Montreal since 1930; she was born in Ontario. She is a free-lance writer and member of the Montreal Writers' Cooperative.

Mary Sachla came to Montreal as a small child, in 1955. She was born in Greece. She is a full-time student at Loyola and works part-time as a clerk.

Rhona Selick is a native Montrealer. She is taking Communication Arts, at Loyola, where she also works part-time.

Catherine Shiff has been living in Montreal for the last 25 years. She holds a B.A. from Hunter College, New York, and an LL.B. from St. John's University. She has two sons and is chairman of the Committee on Canadian Public Affairs of B'nai Brith Women of Montreal.

Katherine E. Waters is a native Montrealer. She holds an Honours B.A. from McGill and an M.A. from Oxford, has two children and teaches English Literature at Loyola. Her special interests are modern British literature and modern poetry.

Shulamith S. Yelen is a native Montrealer. She holds an M.A. from McGill and teaches presently at the Sadie Bronfman Centre. She has one daughter; she writes poetry and criticism. Some of her poems have been published in *Viewpoint*.

Mary Yuill came to Montreal at the age of one, from New Brunswick. She has four daughters, writes poetry, plays the piano, and does volunteer work. She is an evening student at Loyola.

Margret Andersen came to Montreal in 1958, from Berlin, Germany. She holds a Ph.D. from the University of Montreal and teaches French Literature and Women's Studies at Loyola. She has three children, has published several articles, one book, and one language text.

DATE DUE

6. 04 '81	
'5 17'82	
JUN 1 5 1985	
11. 16. '88	
NOV 14 '90	

BRODART, INC.

Cat. No. 23-221

Lewis and Clark College - Watzek Library
HQ1457 .A62   wmain
Andersen, Margret/Mother was not a perso

3 5209 00420 4885